THE REAL
CSI

A Forensic Handbook
for Crime Writers

THE REAL
CSI

A Forensic Handbook
for Crime Writers

KATE BENDELOW

ROBERT HALE

First published in 2017 by Robert Hale,
an imprint of The Crowood Press Ltd,
Ramsbury, Marlborough, Wiltshire SN8 2HR

www. crowood.com

British Library Cataloguing-in-Publication Data
A catalogue record for this book is available from the British
Library.

ISBN 978 0 7198 2228 5

Dedication
For Gary, Sophie and Elissa:
Because we never give up

Typeset by Jean Cussons Typesetting, Diss, Norfolk

Printed and bound in India by Parkson's Graphics

Contents

Preface

I joined Greater Manchester Police (GMP) in 1998 as an income assistant in the finance branch. My aim at that time was to gain a couple more years' life experience whilst familiarizing myself with the structure of GMP, and then apply to become a police constable. Two years later I fell at the first hurdle, as my unaided eyesight was well below the desired limit. Laser eye surgery was still relatively new, and I had neither the courage nor the finances to have it done.

Undefeated, I arranged a meeting with personnel to see what other job opportunities were available for police staff within GMP. Police Community Support Officers (PCSOs) were not introduced until 2002, so my options included enquiry counter staff, communications officer, traffic warden, or crime scene examiner (as a crime scene investigator was then called). This was the first time I had ever heard of the latter role, and the more the personnel officer told me about the job, the more I knew it was the one for me. Part of the essential person specification was to have either a scientific or photographic background, so I quickly enrolled myself on a photographic course at night school.

At the same time, I got to know a couple of the senior crime scene investigators, and was even fortunate enough to go out on attachment with one of their staff. After gaining my photographic qualification in 2002 I successfully applied for the role as a volume crime scene investigator.

I have always been a voracious reader, and as I gained experience in my new career I began to notice a lot of anomalies in the crime fiction I was reading. At the same time, the fictional American crime drama series, *CSI*, had aired in the UK in 2001. This caused what is known as the '*CSI* effect', where over-embellished forensic evidence became regularly portrayed in books, films and television dramas. This effect resulted in jurors and members of the public – and particularly those who became victims of crime – having an unrealistic expectation of how forensic evidence could contribute to a criminal investigation. The fictional account did not live up to the reality by a long way.

At the same time, real crime scene investigators, police officers, solicitors and pathologists were becoming disillusioned and frustrated with the inaccurate portrayal of their work, in the same way that doctors and nurses scorned programmes such as *Casualty*. Although the books and dramas had brilliant, compelling storylines, the obvious inaccuracies did not do the writers the justice they deserved for the amazing pieces of writing they had produced.

In 2013, whilst on maternity leave with my youngest child, I succumbed to my lifelong passion of writing and wrote my first novel, numerous short stories and a succession of poems, some of which I perform at spoken word events. As a result of my writing, I attended the prestigious Swanwick Writer's School in Derbyshire in 2014.

That year forensics officers from Derbyshire Police gave a presentation on a recent murder investigation, detailing how the offender had been brought to justice. It was a fantastic presentation, yet I appreciated the difficulty of giving a police talk to a non-police audience. Although the talk was wonderfully presented, I could see where a lot of my fellow writers were still left with queries about technique, and were baffled by jargon. I volunteered to give a presentation the following year entitled 'Crime Scene Investigation Techniques for Writers'. The feedback from the delegates was overwhelmingly positive, and I recognized a need to provide crime writers with details of forensic procedures that would complement their writing.

As a result I decided to combine my two passions and write this book. Although there are many forensic textbooks available, these are aimed specifically at staff already working in the field, and I wanted to write a book that would provide readers with a succinct guide to crime scene investigation, including the policies and procedures and the emotional impact of working in such a specialized field. Everything you read in this book does not then necessarily have to appear in infinite detail in your own work. Instead, take the information and allow it to infiltrate through your characters where necessary. I hope that the cases referred to throughout this text demonstrate the success of various forensic procedures, as well as providing you with ideas for storylines.

Like any police work, the techniques employed by crime scene investigators during an investigation are long-winded and time-consuming, so it would not be possible to detail all of this in a work of fiction whilst expecting to keep the drama. Time scales can be compressed to keep pace with the storyline as long as there is still an air of accuracy. Also, if you are writing in a particular era, please ensure that the forensic practices you rely on were available during that time period.

It is my hope and intention that crime writers can use this book to add veracity and authenticity to their writing. By having an awareness of factual procedures, writers only need a grain of truth, which can be accurately applied and then manipulated with the twist of fiction.

Only a semblance of truth and experience is needed to give your work the verisimilitude it deserves. Writing is hugely competitive, and crime writing in particular is a crowded genre. I hope this book provides you with the opportunity to access the information you need to complement your writing so it is both successful and accurate.

CHAPTER 1

A Day in the Life of a Real CSI

I have already mentioned the 'CSI effect' and how this has influenced the public's perception regarding the levels of service available to them if they become a victim of crime. In addition, it has provided offenders with an awareness of how to cover their tracks when committing certain crimes in order to avoid detection and identification. The role of a crime scene investigator is one of those few roles that invite people to question how competent you are at your job and to challenge your judgment, which I will illustrate in the following example.

Whilst on duty one day I was asked to examine a car that had been broken into. On arrival at the address, the vehicle's owner told me that he would 'help' me examine the car, as he knew more about my job than I did. When I politely enquired about his credentials he informed me that he owned the full box set of the series *CSI*. Laughing, I complimented him on his sense of humour – only to realize he was deadly serious. He then spent the next forty-five minutes 'helping' me, telling me how to do my job and what I should be looking for, even pointing out that the torch I was using looked like the wrong one. At the same time I tried to convince him that *CSI* is a fictional American television series and not a documentary.

Because victims of crime develop such unrealistic expectations of what can be done for them, this has a negative impact on their relationship with police and can often leave them thinking that we don't care or haven't done enough, which could not be further from the truth. In the vast majority of cases, police officers, police support staff such as PCSOs and crime scene investigators choose to do the job they do because they want to help people and make a difference.

I know how devastating and frustrating it can be for a victim of crime to be told there is nothing that can be done from a policing or forensic perspective to help catch the offender. It is natural for the victim's anger and frustration to then be directed at the officer or the police force as a whole, when the reality is that the offender

'CSI: The Experience': a tourist attraction in Orlando, Florida.

is solely responsible for the offence that has taken place. That is why it is such a wonderful feeling, even after all these years, to discover that the fingerprint or forensic evidence recovered from a crime scene has resulted in the arrest and charge of an offender, be it a murderer or a burglar.

The *CSI* effect is further exacerbated by the financial constraints that are currently putting increased pressure on the police and other emergency services. Such cutbacks mean that every penny spent has to be justified, and the resources available are spread thinner and wider. To ensure that you, as a writer, create characters that reflect the reality of the service provided by today's police forces, we can start by looking at the role of a crime scene investigator, and the different types of crime scene they attend.

THE ROLE OF THE CRIME SCENE INVESTIGATOR

Crime scene investigators used to be known as 'scene of crime officers', or SOCOs for short. This role was first introduced in the United Kingdom in the late sixties, and replaced specialist Criminal Investigation Department (CID) officers with trained civilian personnel. British crime scene investigators are employed by police forces but are civilians and *not* police officers, which is a common misconception held by many members of the public and subsequently some writers. The crime scene investigator's office is usually based within a police station or police HQ.

Because it is a civilian role, crime scene investigators are non-warranted, which means they do not have the power of arrest, nor access to handcuffs, body armour or batons. Crime scene investigators (CSIs) are issued with a police personal radio, CSI uniform and a liveried forensic investigation vehicle. The majority of police forces across the UK have crime scene investigation units that work twenty-four hours a day, seven days a week, or alternatively offer an on-call pager system for major incidents. The CSI units are usually also supported by administrative staff who are an invaluable resource in the smooth running of office operations.

At the start of each shift the crime scene investigator will either be passed any outstanding scene visits from the previous shift, or will monitor the computer or police radio so they are aware when relevant scene visits are reported. These scene visits may be burglaries or more serious incidents that are reported by members of the public. Alternatively, police officers or members of the CID will contact the crime scene investigation unit directly and request a crime scene investigator to attend a scene or examine a piece of evidence.

Senior crime scene investigators oversee any major investigations such as a murder, and are also in charge of the crime scene investigators within their unit. Senior CSIs attend crime scenes either to mentor and train new staff, or to oversee major scene examinations. Prior to closing down a major crime scene, another senior CSI, who has had no previous involvement in the case, will do a final walk-through as a quality-control process to ensure that nothing has been missed or overlooked.

In essence the role of a crime scene investigator is therefore to record, examine and recover evidence from a crime scene. The crime is investigated by police officers, and the recovered evidence is processed and analysed further by other forensic experts such as fingerprint officers. CSIs, like detectives, work as part of a team, therefore the stereotypical lone, maverick investigator is not only a predictable, regurgitated character but is also wholly inaccurate.

To avoid further misconceptions I also need to emphasize that there is nothing glamorous about being a crime scene investigator. The salary won't tempt you to stop doing the lottery, and it isn't always easy working nights, weekends and Christmas rather than being with friends and family. Investigations can be painstaking, back-breaking and at times tedious and very unpleasant. As a writer it is important to recognize this, and to acknowledge that it is the crime scene investigators who work in prolonged, close proximity to the deceased, and not the detectives.

Despite the more difficult scenes, what motivates a crime scene investigator is the fact that it is an amazing, rewarding and worthwhile job. Each shift offers different challenges and also provides an insight into the best and worst of society. The experiences that a CSI will gain in this line of work can be quite unique, as is the camaraderie with colleagues. The role provides an opportunity to help people and make a difference, resulting in overwhelming job satisfaction when an investigation is concluded and offenders have been brought to justice.

Contrary to the role portrayed on *CSI*, real crime scene investigators do not collect the evidence, analyse it, then arrest and interview the suspects. Nor do they have access to a personal-issue firearm or Taser!

VOLUME CRIME

It is important to be aware that crime scene investigators do not spend each shift working with dead bodies – it very much depends on what occurs during each individual's shift. It is not unusual to go several weeks or months without having to deal with a major incident, while at other times it may seem that a major incident occurs on each shift: this 'feast or famine' scenario is typical to police work.

In order to appreciate the type of incident a CSI may be required to attend, I will differentiate between the two crime types. In policing terms, crime is classified as either 'major' or 'volume', and as a result there are two types of crime scene investigators: those who only attend volume crime scenes and those who attend everything, including the major scenes. Volume crime refers to everyday, low-level crime, which, unfortunately, most of us may experience during our lifetime. Volume crime scene investigators deal specifically with these types of incident, which include:

- burglary
- vehicle crime
- theft
- criminal damage
- minor assault injuries

DNA – Then and Now
When I first joined Greater Manchester Police as a volume crime scene investigator in 2002 there was not as much public awareness regarding DNA recovery from crime scenes as there is today. It was quite common to attend burglaries and discover cigarette ends discarded at the scene by offenders, and also fingerprint evidence from a window point of entry or from inside the ignition cowlings of stolen vehicles. Unfortunately modern-day villains tend to be more forensically aware and are careful to cover their tracks, so it is less common these days to find an offender's DNA or fingerprints at a volume crime scene – however, no one is infallible, and many offenders are still caught and brought to justice. You may choose to create characters who are not forensically aware or who are just careless, and therefore *do* leave fingerprints and DNA at a scene.

As a writer, it is also important to be aware that offenders are not just identified through fingerprint or DNA evidence. Chapter 7 will discuss the evidential value of trace evidence, which includes anti-intruder devices such as SmartWater and Smoke Cloak. And bear in mind that many offenders are caught through good old-fashioned policing methods and more basic technology. The following case study highlights how easy it is for the best laid plans to fail.

Case Study: Pride Before a Fall
Aaron was very forensically aware. He took pride in kitting himself out in his burglar's uniform. He wore the most common brand of trainers, which he ensured he changed regularly. He wore leather gloves to avoid leaving fingerprint evidence and because they gave him greater protection near broken glass, therefore minimizing the chances of cutting himself.

He wore a hooded waterproof jacket to avoid shedding fibres, and a scarf that he used to cover his nose and mouth. However, his vanity caught up with him, because just before breaking into the *White Lion* pub he couldn't resist admiring his own reflection in the darkened window as he put on his scarf and carefully arranged his hood, totally unaware that the CCTV cameras were capturing every detail of his not-so-pretty face.

Evidence from Volume Crime Scenes

The types of evidence that volume crime scene examiners will typically look for when examining a scene include fingerprints, DNA and footwear. If an offender has been arrested they may also look for relevant trace evidence: this will be covered in more detail in Chapter 7.

Unless there is a particular health and safety issue, CSIs are not required to wear the customary white paper scene suits typically associated with them when attending a volume crime scene. These are only worn at major crime scenes, as discussed further in Chapter 3. However, when collecting DNA evidence such as saliva or blood from volume crime scenes, CSIs will wear gloves and facemasks.

The Emotional Impact of Volume Crime

At this point it is worth considering that it is not just major crime scenes that can have an emotional effect on investigators or victims: volume crime scenes, particularly burglaries, can also have an impact, especially when it involves vulnerable members of society. Some people find it easier to deal with the aftermath of a burglary by begrudgingly accepting that it is 'one of those things that can happen to anyone' – they do what is needed in practical terms, then put it behind them and move on. In an ideal scenario they will have home insurance to rely on, to replace the items that have been stolen or to repair the damage to doors or windows.

Some burglary victims are understandably more devastated. They take the attack personally, and afterwards live in fear because they feel they and their house have been watched and deliberately targeted: they feel too scared to stay in their home, and at the same time too scared to leave it in case the burglars return. Being in someone's home with them whilst they experience this myriad of emotions can be difficult.

Having to accept that items of overwhelming sentimental value are gone for good can be unbearable. Losing a family heirloom, which carries the memories of generations, probably so the burglar can pay for a bag of drugs adds insult to injury. And think how frustrating it is for the victim, the crime scene investigator and the police officer when no evidence is found at the scene, and there is no CCTV coverage or any other clue that will help find an offender. Imagine how those victims who could not afford home insurance must feel.

In fiction you need to allow your characters to feel these sorts of emotion – and be aware that they will not feel them in isolation. The consequences of crime have a ripple effect on all those concerned, from the victim and the offender to their families and even investigators. Whether a crime is classed as major or volume, the after-effects can never be underestimated – as detailed in the following case study.

Case Study: Aftermath of a Burglary

Mr Aitken had worked for years as a newsagent since returning home after World War II. He had married his childhood sweetheart, and they had been blessed with two children and five grandchildren, their photographs proudly adorning the walls of the lounge. There were also two large display cabinets bursting with precious family memorabilia, including Mr Aitken's war medals, the crystal vase bought for the couple's golden wedding anniversary, and Mrs Aitken's beloved candle-holders.

Sadly, Mrs Aitken had died earlier that year and now, rather than having her by his side, Mr Aitken slept with her photograph on his bedside table. He had threaded her wedding ring through the necklace she always used to wear, and had draped this across the ornate golden picture frame. He took great comfort from the fact that they were next to him whilst he slept.

In the early hours of Tuesday morning a burglar scouring the local area noticed that Mr Aitken's front door was unlocked. He crept in and emptied the contents of both the display cabinets before creeping upstairs and helping himself to the picture frame and jewellery. He also stole a wodge of cash and a watch that Mr Aitken habitually kept under his pillow whilst he slept.

Mr Aitken woke up a few hours later and immediately knew something had happened as the picture frame had gone. He was understandably devastated to realize he had been burgled. He fought back tears as he told me that losing Mrs Aitken's picture and jewellery made him feel as if he had lost her all over again. For the first time in his life, the family home in which he had felt so safe and happy seemed alien and sullied.

I felt terrible when I informed him that despite conducting a painstaking, thorough examination of his property, I had not found any fingerprint or forensic evidence. All I could do was offer words of support, and advise him and his family as to practical crime prevention measures.

His daughter invited him to stay with her for a while, but he felt more scared at the thought of leaving the house than staying in it, in case the burglars returned. Sadly, a week after the burglary Mr Aitken suffered a stroke and died several days later. Prior to this he had been in relatively good health for his age, and his family are in no doubt that the shock of the burglary brought on the stroke.

I hope this case study emphasizes the impact that an everyday crime can have on different people. Can you imagine how disturbing it would be to realize that a burglar had stolen items from under your pillow whilst you slept? It doesn't bear thinking about what else the burglar could potentially have done to someone in such a vulnerable position.

When considering the emotions of your characters, whether they are the victims or the offenders, don't forget to consider how each of them views the police and the policing process, and check if this comes across in their behaviour, responses and dialogue. Are they pro or anti police? Ensure you keep true to your character's feelings towards the police and the effects of crime, rather than your own.

Mishaps at a Crime Scene

Nobody is infallible, and mishaps can quite easily happen at a crime scene, as even investigators are only human. I have yet to watch a programme or read a book that describes how a crime scene investigator is dry-humped by the family's pet Labrador as they bend over to fasten their fingerprint case, or how they arrive at an investigation oblivious to the fact that a pair of knickers is stuck to the Velcro band of the work jacket they hurriedly pulled out of the tumble drier that morning.

I am also quite certain that there is not a single crime scene investigator anywhere who hasn't at some point in their career accidentally fingerprinted the wrong vehicle, caused someone to fall over their misplaced camera kit, broken an exhibit or spilled fingerprint powder during a burglary examination – much to the mortification of themselves and the house-proud home-owner. If you're reading this, Mrs Ashley from Wigan – I would like to apologize once again for the black powder on your beautiful beige rug!

MAJOR CRIME

Now we are aware of what constitutes a volume crime scene, we can look at the offences that are categorized as major crime, as this is what will typically be referred to throughout this book, and is usually the theme adopted by most writers. The types of major crime that a fully trained crime scene investigator will typically work on include:

- murder
- attempted murder
- arson
- rape/sexual assault
- robbery
- drug offences
- high-value fraud
- firearms offences

This list is by no means exhaustive, and crime scene investigators can be called upon to assist in many other reported incidents such as terrorism, kidnap and people trafficking – basically any incident that requires recording photographically, and where assistance with evidence recovery is needed.

Crime scene investigators will work closely with other agencies, depending on the nature of the offence and the location of the crime scene. For example, Social Services may involve the police in neglect cases involving vulnerable members of society, and the scene will then need to be recorded photographically in order to show investigators, and potentially a jury, the extent of the neglect.

Sometimes the homes are in such a dire condition, either covered in excrement or infested with fleas or scabies, that it is necessary to wear a scene suit before entering the address. As it is this type of circumstance that your characters are likely to have to endure, it is worth taking the time to imagine the scenario and how your protagonist would cope in such a situation. For example, is exposure to such regular unpleasantness the driver behind your character's meticulously tidy habits?

Day-to-Day Expectations

Whilst crime scene investigators will be trained in the essentials of the job and may have a scientific background or degree in criminology, there are various personal attributes required for the work that can't be taught or learnt. A successful CSI needs to be a confident and competent communicator; they also need to be quick thinking, innovative and perceptive, as well as having excellent observational skills and an innate ability to be able to interpret what has happened in a crime scene. In order to create a character that is a successful investigator, they will need to have similar attributes.

I have already mentioned how work shifts can range from being fairly quiet with only a few volume crime scenes to examine, or incredibly busy if a major incident such as a murder has occurred: this would involve a number of different scenarios including the murder scene, the deceased, suspects, suspects' houses and vehicles and so on. In order to add accuracy to your writing, it is important to recognize that this is typical of police work. Also consider how your storyline may be affected by the number of people you have on duty, as this is a real consideration faced by police forces across the country in the current financial climate.

Crime scenes can create a plethora of challenging situations, from bad weather affecting the examination of outdoor scenes, bodies situated in cramped or hard-to-reach places, or hazardous scenes such as drugs farms and fire scenes. Although the method of examining a crime scene involves a series of sequential procedures, the scene itself may offer an unprecedented or difficult challenge that has to be adapted or overcome.

Dealing with suspects and victims can also present its own difficulties. Typically, a crime scene investigator will be required to examine suspects or victims and take swabs where appropriate, such as blood from an offender's hands, as well as to record them photographically, which may include having to take close-ups of any obvious blood staining or injuries.

It is possible that the victim or suspect may be distressed, angry or aggressive, and dealing with someone in this state in close proximity can be a challenging experience for your characters. There may be a language barrier, or no communication at all, particularly if the suspect is intent on using their right to remain silent; this in itself can be quite frustrating or even unnerving. Also consider that the individual may not be able to stay still during examination, through pain, agitation or withdrawal, or simply because they have no intention of being cooperative!

It is important to think about the types of situation your characters may be faced with. The reality is that the current portrayal of crime scene investigators, both on screen and in books, tends to be more glamorized than it is in real life. Be aware of the unpleasant situations faced by investigators: it is not just dead bodies that smell – living, breathing suspects and victims do too, and so do their homes!

FROM CRIME SCENE INVESTIGATOR TO CHARACTER

Now you are aware of the types of incident that crime scene investigators and police officers will attend, start to think of how your characters would cope in various situations. For a character to be believable it is essential that writers bring them to life vividly and are able to portray them accurately to the reader, warts and all.

I have already mentioned how the impact of crime has a ripple effect on all those involved. Furthermore, no single person knows how they will cope with a life-changing, unprecedented incident until they are in that situation. People who are normally calm and reasonable can become aggressive, dangerous and unpredictable, and vice versa, therefore crime writers are more challenged by having to anticipate how their victims or offenders will react. Add into the mix the reaction of loved ones and investigators involved in the storyline, and a myriad of unexpected emotions must be considered.

Start by imagining how your characters – whether they are victim, offenders, investigators or loved ones – would react to the sight and smells of a crime scene. The sudden discovery of a dead body or the bloody aftermath of a violent assault can seem quite surreal, and this sensation can act as a buffer to the emotions the individual is experiencing at that time. Is their overriding reaction going to be one of flight or fight? Will they have the composure and ability to administer first aid if it's relevant, or to ensure a scene is protected? Has your character actually been at the crime scene, or have they just been told about it?

Which would be worse to that character: to witness the scene at first hand, or having to imagine it from the jagged pieces of information that gradually emerge? For me, a crime scene that is described to me sounds worse than when I actually see it for myself, as my imagination tends to go into overdrive.

Would it be more devastating to be the loved one of a murder victim or of a murderer? If the character is an investigator, how do they cope with working for hours on end in uncomfortable, cramped conditions in extremes of temperature? What are their weak points? What disturbs them the most: hands-on contact with a dead body, or the smell?

Maybe there are other issues that even the toughest investigator finds distressing. For example, some can cope with assault on, or the murder of children, but can't deal with anything involving harm to animals. So would that character be able to 'switch off' from the case they have been working on, or is there something about that particular incident that for them is particularly disturbing, or even motivating?

If the character is a victim, do they react with anger and demand retribution, or will the fear and injury they have sustained cause them to become a shadow of their former selves, possibly causing a loved one to seek retribution on their behalf?

Consider the devastating effect of grief, which can become all-encompassing and may consume an individual to the point of insanity. Would such grief act as a motivator, inducing thoughts of hatred or revenge, or would it cause the person to shut down and withdraw? Losing a loved one is bad enough, but to lose someone in violent, tragic circumstances becomes even more unbearable and unfathomable.

Whatever the circumstances or the character, take time as a writer to imagine the incident, and put yourself in that position or at that crime scene. In your imagination expose each of your senses to what has taken place, either as a victim, witness or offender. Don't hold back: be scared, angry – incensed even! Allow yourself to feel every conceivable emotion, including perhaps the cold, detached, unemotional response of the attacker. By appreciating the various crime types and by allowing yourself to imagine that crime scene, you can add an extra dimension to your characters, and this will be felt by your readers.

Write cleverly and use what you have learnt, imagined and experienced to build up the power of suggestion, which your readers' imagination will then elaborate on. Do your nightmares unnerve you more than horror films? Think why, and transpose the elements of what most disturbs you into your own storyline. Write suggestively, however, rather than using long, over-descriptive accounts of violence.

Be a responsible writer and take the time to craft your scenes so they are sinister rather than morbidly detailed – I personally believe that going into too much detail when writing about sexual violence, for example, can potentially fuel a perverse mind. Think about your readers: if they have experienced such an ordeal in real life, the last thing they need is for the comfort and safety of their own home to be compromised by reading about, or watching, something similar. Such disturbing events can be hinted at, and don't need to be spelled out in detail – and don't underestimate the power of the imagination: it is more than capable of filling in the blanks.

Also remember that if *you* don't get emotionally involved in, or even unnerved by, what you are writing, then neither will your readers. Revel in the darkness of your chosen genre, let the events unfold, and then arm yourself with a team of efficient investigators and the knowledge of how a crime scene is examined to bring your narrative to a realistic and plausible conclusion, the impact of which will stay with your readers long after your story has been told.

CHAPTER 2

Dealing with Death

One of the questions that crime scene investigators are commonly asked is how they cope when working on particularly unpleasant crime scenes, and in particular when having to examine and handle dead bodies. I suppose the answer is that it is simply a requirement of the job, and the focus is on doing what is necessary at each crime scene to bring offenders to justice, rather than dwelling on any emotional aspect.

I have always been one of those people who can remember their dreams every night, and have always been prone to nightmares. Since working as a crime scene investigator, the sights and smells I am exposed to during my shift do not immediately bother me, but they do seem to add fuel to my very vivid imagination, resulting in even worse nightmares. My subconscious mind is obviously more affected than my conscious mind, which could be why I am naturally drawn towards writing 'dark' fiction.

In the majority of cases, crime scene investigators do not have to deal with the victim's family, and this can make a huge difference: speaking personally, being exposed to their emotional distress would be unbearable to me, whereas I am quite comfortable in the knowledge that as far as the deceased is concerned, nothing else can hurt them. I have spoken to doctors and nurses who are disturbed at the thought of having to examine dead bodies, in the same way that I couldn't cope with dealing with people in pain and suffering.

Having 'gallows humour' helps enormously. While this coping mechanism is in no way disrespectful to the victims or their families, it is a practical reaction to having to deal with stressful and traumatic situations. The reality is that the level of crime and violence witnessed on a daily basis becomes normality for people working in such an environment, so don't be afraid to let your characters display their black humour.

Something else that crime scene investigators usually get asked about is the smell associated with dead bodies. The smell of death is unique and unforgettable, and trying to describe it does not always quite measure up to first-hand experience. It is an overwhelming, thick and pungent odour you can almost taste – the stench is so strong it almost feels 'heavy' to the senses, like a gas or vapour. It has a sickeningly sweet undertone, like acetone, which mingles with the foetid smell of decay, similar to sewage. The smell emanating from an animal-rendering plant is similar and a good way of exposing yourself to this kind of smell.

If the deceased has been taking drugs, whether prescription or illegal, this can also affect the smell of the body, because once decomposition begins, the chemical compound is released, and this can result in an unbearable, gaseous stench similar to ammonia. Also, if the body has been burnt in a fire, the deceased will smell of charring, not dissimilar to the smell of barbecued meat, since effectively that is what it is.

When creating a crime scene, always consider the location of the body. Rarely is the deceased left lying on their back in the middle of a large field with a knife protruding neatly from their chest. People can die in the most inconvenient, difficult-to-reach places such as on the toilet or in a derelict, unsafe building. Bodies can be stuffed in wheelie bins, suitcases or wardrobes, and found in chest freezers, loft spaces or under beds.

In fiction, body location is important in order to maintain a level of reality, as you will need to consider how the body will be moved or transported. Ideally it takes two healthy adults to carry a cadaver, as it is quite literally a dead weight that is difficult to manoeuvre. Also consider the posture of the deceased: if, for example, they are discovered in a cramped condition during rigor mortis, it will be

Bodies can be difficult to dispose of.

difficult to straighten out the cadaver, and it will be awkward to carry, disguise or dispose of it.

The body's state of decomposition must also be considered: this will depend on how long it has been in situ and the conditions in which it is lying. I have already attempted to describe the foul smell that accompanies death: now add decomposition into the mix and the situation becomes much worse.

THE STAGES OF DECOMPOSITION

The decomposition process is recognized as occurring in several stages following death; these stages are known as:

- pallor mortis
- algor mortis
- rigor mortis
- cadaveric spasm
- lividity
- putrefaction
- decomposition
- skelotonization

Pallor Mortis

Pallor mortis is the first stage of death, which occurs once blood stops circulating in the body. The cessation of an oxygenated blood flow to the capillaries beneath the skin causes the deceased to pale in appearance. In non-Caucasians the pallor may appear to develop an unusual hue; the skin will lose any natural lustre and appears more waxen. Pallor mortis occurs quite quickly, within about ten minutes after death.

Algor Mortis

Algor mortis is the term given to the cooling of the body after death. The cooling process will be influenced by many factors, including the deceased's clothing; it is described in further detail below, when we discuss how to determine the time of death.

Rigor Mortis

Rigor mortis is the stage that people probably consider the most when thinking about the effects of death on a body. Rigor mortis can occur between two and six hours after death, although factors including temperature can greatly affect this. It is caused by the muscles partially contracting, and the lack of aerobic respiration means that the muscles cannot relax from the contraction, leaving them tense, subsequently resulting in the stiffening we associate with rigor mortis.

This stage typically begins in the head, starting with the eyes, mouth, jaw and neck, and progresses right through the body. The process is concluded approximately twelve hours after death (although, again, certain variables may occur) and lasts between twenty-four and seventy-two hours depending on circumstances.

Contrary to popular belief, rigor mortis is not a permanent state and is in fact reversed, with the muscles relaxing in the same order in which they initially stiffened. The reversing process also takes approximately twelve hours, when the body returns to its un-contracted state.

It is possible to 'break' rigor mortis by manipulating and flexing the limbs. This is usually done by undertakers, pathologists or crime scene investigators who are attempting to examine or move a body – or by a murderer trying to hide their victim in the closet or the boot of a car.

Cadaveric Spasm

Cadaveric spasm is a phenomenon that can be misinterpreted as rigor mortis; it can also spark the imagination of any self-respecting crime writer. This condition is the instantaneous stiffening of the body (most commonly the hands) following a traumatic death. Unlike rigor mortis, the stiffening of the affected limb is permanent and is not reversed, causing the deceased to maintain the rigidity until such time as putrefaction causes breakdown of the particular muscle group.

Cadaveric spasm may occur following a fatal air crash; in one example the deceased were later discovered still clutching their seatbelts or arm rests in a final, desperate act of survival. In a drowning case, the victim was discovered with grass from the riverbank still grasped in their hand. Perhaps the most famous case of cadaveric spasm involves the rock band Nirvana's lead singer, Kurt Cobain.

Cobain reportedly committed suicide in April 1994. His body was discovered a few days after his death with a shotgun wound to the head, and tests revealed he had large traces of heroin in his system. He was reportedly discovered still clutching the gun in his left hand, due to cadaveric spasm. However, a great deal of controversy surrounds the veracity of this latter assumption, and indeed the cause of his death, with many people insisting and attempting to prove that he died as the result of foul play rather than suicide.

Lividity

The lividity stage is also known as livor mortis or hypostasis. Once blood can no longer circulate, it will gravitate towards the lowest point of the body. For example, a supine body will display pinkish/purple patches of discoloration where the blood has settled in the back and along the thighs. Lividity occurs about thirty minutes after death, but will not necessarily be noticeable until at least two hours afterwards as the pooling process intensifies and becomes visible, finally peaking up to between eight and twelve hours later.

Once it is complete, the lividity process cannot be reversed. Therefore a body discovered lying on its side, but with staining evident in the back and shoulders, must have been moved at some point from what would have been a supine position at the time of death.

It is worth noting that if the body has had contact with the floor, a wall or other solid surface, lividity would not occur at the points of contact as the pressure would not allow the blood to seep through the capillaries and pool. The specific area of pressure will be the same colour as the rest of the body and a pattern of contact may well be evident.

Putrefaction

We now reach the most unpalatable stage following death. The word 'putrefaction' derives from the Latin *putrefacere*, meaning 'to make rotten' – which certainly understates its effects! The body becomes rotten through the process known as autolysis, which is the liquefaction of bodily tissue and organs and the breakdown of proteins within the body due to the increased presence of bacteria.

The first visible sign of this process is the discoloration of the skin in the area of the abdomen. Bacteria released from the intestine cause the body to become bloated with a mixture of gases; over time these will leak out, and the smell will intensify to unbearable proportions. Typically this will attract flies, which will lay eggs, which develop into maggots – and lots of them! Bloating is most evident in the stomach area, genitals and face, which can become unrecognizable as the tongue and eyes are forced to protrude due to the pressure of the build-up of gases in the body. At this stage the body will also begin to lose hair.

The organs typically decompose in a particular order, starting with the stomach, followed by the intestines, heart, liver, brain, lungs, kidney, bladder and uterus/prostate. Once all the gases have escaped the skin begins to turn black: this stage is called 'black putrefaction'. As with all the other stages of death so far, the rate of putrefaction depends on temperature and location. A body exposed to the air above ground will decompose more quickly than a body left in water or buried below ground.

During putrefaction, blistering of the skin and fermentation can also occur. Fermentation refers to a type of mould that will grow on the surface of the body. This mould appears white, and is slimy or furry in texture. It also releases a very strong, unpleasant, cheesy smell.

As the putrefaction process comes to an end, fly and maggot activity will become less, which leads to the next stage: decomposition.

Decomposition

The body is an organic substance comprising organisms that can be broken down by chemical decomposition. If the body is outside, any remains that have not been scavenged or consumed by maggots will liquefy and seep into the surrounding soil: thus when the body decomposes it is effectively recycled and returned to nature.

Skelotonization

The final stage of death is known as 'dry decay', when the cadaver has all but dried out: the soft tissue has all gone and only the skeleton remains. If the cadaver is outside, not only is it exposed to the elements but it also becomes food for scavengers such as rats, crows or foxes. As the remains are scavenged, the body parts become dispersed so it is not unusual to find skeletal remains some distance from where the body lay at the point of death. The way in which skeletal remains are scattered in such cases is of interest to archaeologists, and is referred to as taphonomy.

Where a body has lain undiscovered at home for a period of time it has also been known for family pets, typically dogs, to feed on the body. The natural instinct of a pet is to attempt to arouse the deceased by licking them, but once it gets hungry, its survival instinct will take over and it will consider the body as little more than carrion: it will act with the same natural instinct as a scavenger in the wild, which will feed on any corpse, be it animal or human, if it is starving. Obviously the number of pets, the body mass of the deceased and the time lapse before the body is discovered will influence to what extent it has been devoured.

For further research on the stages of decomposition and the factors that affect it, search the internet for information on body farms. These are medical facilities where bodies are donated for research purposes so scientists can specifically observe the decomposition process. However, be aware that some of the images are quite graphic. There are currently no body farms in the UK or anywhere in Europe, but at least half a dozen operate in the USA.

DETERMINING THE TIME OF DEATH

In real-life murder investigations and compelling crime fiction, time of death is an essential piece of the jigsaw when establishing a timeline of events. Each stage of decomposition can be given an approximate time scale, which may help pinpoint the time of death, but as already mentioned, there are many variables that can affect the accuracy of this calculation.

Take, for example, temperature as a determining factor – this can be measured using a calculation known as the Glaister equation. This formula measures the hourly reduction in the body's core temperature to calculate the time of death. However, the cooling process of the body can vary depending on the type of clothing the deceased is wearing, or whether they are covered with bed linen such as blankets or duvets.

The body will typically cool to the ambient room temperature, but this obviously alters if there is heating in the room or if there is a constant draught cooling the body. Also, a body left outside in extreme weather conditions will not conform to the Glaister equation due to the external influence of the climate it is exposed to.

There are other variables in using temperature as a determining factor. For example, a body with greater mass will cool at a slower rate than someone who was slim and frail. Disease and drugs are also an important factor in body temperature. It is also believed that a body that has haemorrhaged will cool much more quickly as a result. Trauma can also have an effect – an act such as asphyxiation can cause an increase in body temperature. If the deceased has been involved in a prolonged, rigorous fight prior to death, then again, their body temperature is likely to be increased at time of death.

Because there are so many variables it is not possible for a pathologist to provide a time of death – they will only ever be able to provide an estimation, and even this should be noted with caution. Investigators will consider other information, such as the deceased's last known movements, gathered from interviews with neighbours, colleagues and loved ones in order to establish who last saw the victim alive – yet even this is not foolproof.

I once examined the putrefying remains of a male whose neighbours were adamant they had seen him that same morning. They recalled the brief conversation they had had with him as he returned from the corner shop, clutching his newspaper and some milk. The presence of an unopened newspaper dated seven weeks prior to the police discovery, and the fact that I was staring into the cavity that used to be his stomach, quickly dispelled their claims.

Mobile phone activity, including the use of social media, also cash transactions and CCTV footage can all help provide a timeline of events for the deceased, and indeed any alibies for suspects – that is, of course, if it *is* the victim or suspect who has used the relevant medium and not someone attempting to cover their traces. If a body is recovered years after time of death, then clothing, jewellery and coinage that may be recovered on, or with it, could become useful lines of enquiry when attempting to determine the time of death.

FEATURES OF DEATH

There are certain causes of death, or conditions that prevail during the decomposition process, that may cause the body to take on an unusual appearance or to deviate from the expected state of decomposition. These can include:

- drowning
- fire (charring)
- mummification
- carbon monoxide poisoning

Drowning

Drowning can be accidental, murder or suicide. Dumping a body in water may be a murderer's attempt to dispose of it in the hope that it will remain undiscovered or to degrade any tell-tale DNA or trace evidence. It is possible for the pathologist to ascertain if death has been caused by drowning or if the person was already dead before entering the water. The presence of diatoms in the body indicates that death was caused by drowning.

Diatoms are a type of single-celled algae unique to the body of water they are found in; this may be saltwater or freshwater, and from a specific lake or estuary. They are not present in tap water as it is filtered, and therefore will not be present in somebody who has drowned in a bath, although water present in the stomach and lungs of the deceased is still indicative of death by drowning.

Diatoms can only enter the body by being ingested through the lungs or stomach of a living person while the heart is still beating. Their presence will then be discovered in the blood, bone marrow and brain of the deceased. When attending water deaths, a water sample will be taken so the diatoms present in the source can be compared to those identified in the body. In this way, investigators can ascertain whether the victim was drowned in the same body of water in which it was discovered.

Bodies that have been immersed in water for any length of time are likely to be discovered in a macerated form. This is when the skin wrinkles and loosens to such an extent that it starts to become detached. The skin may also appear adipocerous: this is when a wax-like coating progressively covers the body when it is overexposed to wet conditions. Adipocere is caused by the reaction of body fat to water; hydrolysis occurs, resulting in the coagulation of fat, which spreads across the surface of exposed areas of the body.

Vagal drowning occurs when the vagus nerves become unintentionally over-stimulated, resulting in a cardiac arrest. The vagus nerves serve the lungs, heart, chest and abdomen. Cardiac arrest can occur when the body is suddenly exposed to cold water, which causes vagal inhibition, particularly when cold water suddenly enters the larynx or ears, or strikes the abdomen in the event of the person falling into water. This instantaneous reaction leaves a person incapacitated, and is potentially the cause of many deaths of people who are under the influence of drink or drugs and behave without due care and attention when close to canals and waterways. Inhibition of the vagal nerve can also occur during asphyxiation.

Fire (Charring)

After drowning, I personally think that the second worse way to die is in a fire or through smoke inhalation. As with drowning, this process can also be an opportunity for murderers to dispose of cumbersome corpses before they succumb to the unpleasantness of decomposition. Again, pathologists will be able to ascertain if the victim was dead before the fire by examining the lungs and airways to detect the presence of soot.

If a body has been assaulted prior to the fire, it is possible for pathologists to detect signs of an assault by examining the skeletal remains. Even if the body is severely blackened through charring, it can still provide pathologists with much needed clues. Another indication that a person has been assaulted prior to the fire is the lack of what is called 'pugilistic pose' in the body.

The description 'pugilistic pose' is taken from a boxing stance where the fighter stands with clenched fists and arms, and legs flexed in a particular defensive position. During a fire, the intense heat causes the hands, elbows and knees to flex and stiffen, drawing the body into this recognized position. If, however, the victim was assaulted before the fire, then damage to the joints will prevent the body adopting the pugilist position.

Dead bodies are therefore capable of providing many clues.

Mummification

A body may *not* decompose depending on certain circumstances. For example, bodies kept in extremely cold conditions will not succumb to bacteria or insect activity. The Lindow Man is one of many preserved bodies recovered from peat bogs across the United Kingdom: his remains were discovered by peat cutters working on Lindow Moss, Cheshire in 1984. Experts have concluded that he died a violent death between 2BC and AD119 and his body has been preserved for the ensuing centuries due to the cool temperature, low oxygenation and high acidity of the peat bog.

Following death, some bodies may not succumb to the decomposition process because they become mummified. In order for this state to occur the body must be exposed to a stable temperature (preferably warm) with a steady air current, which allows the body to dry out. The desert is an obvious choice of environment to promote mummification, but the right combination of elements nearer to home has also produced the same effect.

In Germany in 1994, police discovered the mummified remains of a lady who they believe had died of natural causes six months earlier. She was discovered in her lounge in front of the television, and neighbours only thought to raise the alarm after noticing that her letterbox was overflowing with post. The lady's body was most likely mummified due to the constant temperature of her room over such a long period of time.

Carbon Monoxide Poisoning

The introduction of unleaded petrol and catalytic converters in cars has led to a decline in the typical suicide scenario of a desperate person sitting in their car with the engine running and a hosepipe threaded through the window. Even so, carbon monoxide is still very much a killer due to faulty gas pipes and damaged heaters and fires.

The early symptoms of carbon monoxide poisoning can be similar to flu, but increased exposure to the gas, as well as old age and failing health, can prove fatal to the victim. One of the noticeable, distinct features of a person who has died as a result of carbon monoxide poisoning is cherry reddening of the skin. We know that in normal circumstances in the first stage of death there is a noticeable paling of the skin due to algor mortis, therefore this distinctive reddening is an obvious sign that death has not occurred due to natural causes.

BLOOD LOSS AND STAINING

Having considered the various stages of decomposition, there is still an element of death that some people find unpalatable: blood. If you knock over a cup of coffee it seems to spill everywhere, pooling on the floor as well as splashing up the wallpaper, and takes a long time to clean up. A coffee cup holds about twelve fluid ounces: the average adult human body contains approximately eight pints of blood, so you can start to imagine the amount of blood potentially discovered at a crime scene and how difficult it may be clean up; this will be discussed in more detail in Chapter 5.

Once again, to write with accuracy and to avoid misrepresentation of your crime scene, how your victim is attacked will impact upon the extent of the blood splatter. For example, if a character is stabbed, the puncture wound may appear relatively insignificant compared to the internal damage caused, and in such a case there may not be too much external blood loss. If your victim has been shot in the head with a pistol, there will be less damage than if they were shot in the head with a shotgun.

If the character has been slashed with a sharp instrument, the wound will be larger and more obvious, and will result in heavier blood staining. If a character has been stabbed in an area that causes an arterial bleed, your crime scene will resemble something from a horror scene, as the blood will spurt out quickly and is most likely to cause death.

Other factors should also be borne in mind: alcohol has an effect as it thins the blood, which will result in an increase in blood loss. Lacerations are caused by blunt objects, and incisions by a stab wound. If a body sustains puncture wounds after death, then blood loss tends to be restricted to a low seepage similar to a leak, as the heart will have ceased its pumping function. A pathologist will be able to ascertain whether injuries have been sustained before or after death.

CHAPTER 3

Crime Scene Preservation

Imagine that your crime scene is like a brand new car: picture that perfect, gleaming paintwork, the crisp interior, and of course that distinctive new-car smell. Now, who are you going to allow into your new vehicle: are you happy to just offer a stranger on the street a lift? Your friend has just finished decorating and wants to borrow your new car, but their clothes are covered in dust, plaster and paint – are you happy for them to drive it like this and compromise its integrity or would you want them to get changed?

Like your new car, your crime scene is precious and it is important to preserve its integrity: we should therefore consider the procedures involved in ensuring that a crime scene is preserved correctly so that your writing is accurate and realistic, and that you avoid the common pitfalls that many unresearched writers fall into. By considering the effects of preservation, writers can also plausibly suggest how vital evidence can be missed or destroyed, in ways relevant to their storyline.

The process of examining a crime scene involves identifying it, securing it and protecting it until such time as all the evidence has been recovered, and it is agreed that the scene can be released. The senior investigating officer (SIO) is typically a detective inspector (DI) or detective chief inspector (DCI). They are fundamentally responsible for the investigation and will continue to advise ranks above them, such as the superintendent, as to how the case is progressing. The SIO will work closely with the crime scene manager as well as managing their own team of detectives.

The SIO and crime scene manager will agree a forensic strategy that will take into account the initial crime scene and any peripheral scenes as and when they are discovered, such as suspects and their houses and vehicles. The crime scene manager will then task crime scene investigators accordingly. Ideally, the same crime scene investigator will remain with the crime scene until it is concluded, but operational demands, such as staffing levels, can mean that this is not always possible.

IDENTIFYING A CRIME SCENE

Once the police are aware, or suspect, that a crime has taken place, the first officer in attendance will ensure that the scene is identified and secured. Identification sounds obvious, but it is possible to make mistakes due to an inaccurate witness or time scale, or human error.

If your crime scene contains a smoking gun and a body in situ, then it is fairly obvious that you have the correct location. However, if your crime scene is historic, how certain are you that your characters have located the right scene? How accurate is your character's recollection? Can your witnesses be trusted – do they have an alternative motive? Is the location of the body the murder scene or a dumping site?

The rank of the first officer in attendance will typically be a uniformed police constable, because they are the response officers who will reply to the emergency call that comes to the police control room via 999. In the event that a body is then discovered at the scene, it is necessary to confirm that life is extinct. At this stage the uniformed officers will liaise with CID officers to establish if the death is to be treated as suspicious or not.

Confirmation of Death

On 9 July 1997 in the village of Chillenden in Kent, Lin Russell and her daughters Josie and Megan were tied up and beaten with a hammer during a failed robbery attempt by killer, Michael Stone. Police officers who attended the horrific scene failed to find any signs of life from the three females and their family dog Lucy, and the murder investigation began.

Over an hour later, when the police surgeon, Dr Parks, attended the scene, PC Leivers, who had been one of the first responding officers, noticed that the position of nine-year-old Josie's body had moved. PC Leivers alerted Dr Parks, who discovered that, although Josie was unconscious and very badly beaten, her body was warm and still showing signs of life. Despite suffering life-changing injuries, Josie survived and was able to provide a witness statement and piece together events surrounding the murders.

This tragic event highlights the importance of a medical expert attending a crime scene and confirming death. Unless the death is obvious, such as the victim's head lying three feet away from its torso, then it is essential to allow a paramedic, a doctor or a police surgeon to attend the crime scene.

Medical Intervention and Scene Preservation

Crime writers often want to know if medical intervention is detrimental to a crime scene. The answer is 'possibly', but preservation of life is, and always will be, the fundamental priority in any situation. The fact of paramedics working on a person who has been assaulted, shot or stabbed could potentially result in the loss of fragile trace evidence. However, the potential value of that trace evidence is inconsequential when compared to the value of a life.

I have attended deaths, mainly suicides, where paramedics have covered the deceased with a blanket. Although I appreciate that this is done out of respect for the deceased, the reality is that it introduces more evidence into the scene. It is also not unusual to discover disposable gloves at a scene, discarded by the first officer attending, or paramedics or doctors. Carelessly leaving items at a scene in this way, particularly so close to the body, can be very frustrating for the CSI, particularly if there is no way of confirming whether the gloves belonged to the officers or the murderer.

Establishing if Death is Suspicious

If the first officers responding to the report of a death observe a knife protruding from the victim's chest, then it is safe to say that the death should be treated as suspicious. But not all deaths are so obvious, so how do police establish if a sudden death is to be treated as suspicious or not? This can depend on many factors, including the location, initial appearance and posture of the body, the victim's age, medical history and lifestyle, or if they have incurred recent police involvement or have a history of violence.

One of the first measures taken by the police when attending an unexpected death is to inform the coroner. The coroner will have a background in either medicine or law, and their job is to oversee the investigation into deaths that have occurred suddenly (by unknown means or unnaturally), violently, or whilst the victim was in police or prison custody. Once notified of the death the coroner will officially open and then adjourn an inquest, allowing the police to conduct their investigation.

Signs of a disturbance where the deceased is located, or obvious signs of violence on the body, provide a strong indication of foul play. Other scenes may not be so easy to interpret – there may be some subtle sign at a seemingly obvious suicide that may attract the attention of the attending investigators, or unexplained bruising on the body of a bed-bound pensioner. In other cases, babies and adults can sadly die due to natural causes such as sudden death syndrome, a condition that may not have been predicted or prevented (although there are clear NHS guidelines given to help reduce the risk of sudden infant death syndrome in babies).

The discovery of such sudden deaths will be treated as potentially suspicious until such time as investigators and the coroner are satisfied that there is no possibility of foul play. This approach is taken to ensure that any potential evidence is not compromised: once people have trampled through a scene, the evidence cannot be put back. The scene may well be preserved and left until after the post mortem has been conducted, then if the results of the post mortem reveal that there is no evidence of foul play, and a legitimate cause of death is found, there is no need to conduct a crime scene investigation and the property can be released.

Fatal (or life-changing) works accidents will also be investigated by the police in order to establish a sequence of events, and to rule out any third party involvement. At this stage the Health and Safety Executive (HSE) will also be notified, and once the police are satisfied that there is no criminal element to the death, the HSE will take responsibility for conducting the investigation and will report their findings to the coroner's court. A corporation, organization, department, police force or employer can be prosecuted under the Corporate Manslaughter and Corporate Homicide Act, 2007 (CMCHA) for breaching legislation, which states:

(1) An organisation to which this section applies is guilty of an offence if the way in which its activities are managed or organised
   a) causes a person's death, and
   b) amounts to a gross breach of a relevant duty of care owed by the organisation to the deceased.

Section 1, CMCHA, 2007

Being found guilty of corporate manslaughter can result in a very large fine or even a custodial sentence. Crime scene investigators may be asked to attend the scene of work accidents to record it photographically or to video it, and to assist in seizing or packaging any relevant pieces of potential evidence for the police or for HSE purposes.

The Post Mortem

If a death is deemed suspicious then a post mortem (PM), also known as an autopsy, will be conducted by a Home Office (HO) pathologist. A Home Office post mortem differs from a standard PM, as particular consideration is given to recovering forensic evidence and to the investigation of injuries inflicted on victims of violent death, stabbings and shootings. The job of the pathologist is to establish how, when and why a person has died, as well as gathering information regarding diseases or other medical conditions, such as sudden infant death syndrome, mentioned above. The collating of such evidence at a post mortem has been an integral part of finding a cure or initiating procedures for prevention.

When somebody has been involved in a fatal stabbing, often members of the general public cannot comprehend why a PM is necessary, as surely the cause of death is obviously due to the stabbing? Murder investigations, however, are not so straightforward, and it is the job of the HO pathologist to catalogue the injuries the victim has sustained in order to illustrate, where necessary, how frenzied the attack was.

They will also be able to ascertain which one of the many stab wounds delivered the fatal blow and what the actual cause of death was, whether a stab wound to the heart, or internal bleeding from a ruptured spleen. These are questions the police, coroner, prosecution, defence and, most of all, the family, all need answers to. A thorough medical investigation is needed in order to rule out any other possible scenarios – for instance, it may transpire that the victim of the stabbing actually died as a result of having been poisoned: this is by no means far-fetched fiction, it can actually happen.

As with any other stage of a crime scene investigation, the post mortem is photographed throughout, with the photographer concentrating on close-ups of scars, tattoos, bruising and lacerations. This is the job of the CSI or imaging specialist, depending on resources and individual force practice. If the CSI is required to take photographs, then it is likely that another CSI will attend to assist in taking body samples from the pathologist. The rationale behind this is that the CSI who is photographing is the 'clean' CSI, left in charge of the camera, rather than having physical contact with the deceased, which is the task of the 'dirty' CSI.

Other people expected to be present obviously include the pathologist, an exhibits officer (part of CID, responsible for collecting and collating all evidence from the numerous scenes involved in the investigation), another member of the murder investigation team, and possibly the SIO, who may choose to watch the proceedings from a purpose-built viewing room whilst continuing to coordinate the investigation.

The types of sample taken very much depend on the condition of the body and the circumstances surrounding the death, but generally the pathologist will take the following:

- hair combings and/or plucked head hair
- facial hair (including eyebrows and eyelashes)
- nasal swabs
- mouth swabs
- nail clippings/scrapings
- body hair
- pubic hair
- penile or vaginal swabs
- anal swabs
- vitreous humor sample
- blood samples for DNA and toxicology
- urine sample
- stomach contents

Any bite marks on the body will also be photographed and swabbed. If the victim has been attacked with a weapon that has then been located, it is useful for the pathologist either to see it, or to be presented with photographs taken to scale so they can make comparisons between the weapon and the deceased's injuries. In the case of shooting incidents, the pathologist will locate and remove the bullet (if it is still present within the body) and will attempt to illustrate its trajectory if it has passed through other organs or body parts.

The pathologist will remove and weigh each organ in turn, and will retain possible samples for further testing, depending on the nature of the death. Once the post mortem is concluded, the pathologist will return all the organs to the body and the mortician will stitch the body back together and wash it. At this point fingerprints can be taken for identification or comparison purposes. The deceased's family may be allowed to view the body, if it is considered appropriate, so that it can be formally identified, if this has not already been done.

It is possible for a secondary post mortem to be conducted as part of the murder investigation. If arrests have been made, the defence solicitor can request their own pathologist to conduct a secondary examination of the deceased to allow them to confirm or refute the original findings. After a certain time, if nobody has been arrested and there is subsequently no defence team to request this, then the coroner will ask for a secondary, independent pathologist to conduct the PM, and their findings will be retained for future purposes. This allows the coroner to then authorize the release of the body back to the family so a funeral can be arranged.

A Home Office post mortem can take between three and six hours depending on the nature of death, the condition of the body and the severity of the injuries. The first post mortem I attended was a lady whose death was not thought to be suspicious. A medical post mortem had been partially conducted at the hospital but then stopped, as the pathologist was concerned about some internal bruising they had noticed.

I was still quite new to the job and had gone to the post mortem for the experience. The examination room reminded me of the clinical, disinfectant-smelling environment of old Victorian swimming baths, the tiled room causing an echoing effect that made me feel slightly disoriented and nervous. However, I was soon watching with fascination as the post mortem continued, and the HO pathologist took time to explain the various stages and samples that were being taken and tested. For me, this post mortem represented a huge learning curve.

A case of particular significance was that of former GP Harold Shipman. In January 2000 Shipman was found guilty at Preston Crown Court of the murder of fifteen of his former patients; he was also suspected of being responsible for the deaths of another 218. Shipman's case is significant because it led to a fundamental review of medical practices. Dame Janet Smith DBE held an enquiry, and her recommendations came into practice in 2009, so that now, when a GP issues a death certificate, relatives wishing to arrange a cremation require a second doctor to complete a certificate confirming death.

Other circumstances may also require a post mortem. There may be certain reasons why a doctor cannot provide a death certificate; for example the victim may have died unexpectedly, without seeing their family GP within the last fourteen days. And if a person dies having only just been admitted to hospital the cause of death will probably not be known. In such cases the death will be reported to the coroner, who may then request a medical post mortem to ascertain the cause of death.

SECURING THE CRIME SCENE

Once the crime scene is identified, police officers will ensure that any people present, including suspects, witnesses and paramedics, are removed to ensure that the crime scene cannot be disturbed or altered. The same applies if there are pets at the scene – it would be seriously unhelpful if the pet dog were to start licking blood off the murder weapon, which can happen.

Once everyone is removed from the scene, the next people to enter will be the crime scene investigators. It is important to bear this in mind, as many writers mistakenly hand over their crime scene at this point to their lead detective: in their fiction the detective will then trample throughout the scene, searching, handling and even removing evidence, only later allowing the faceless CSI to come in to conduct a cursory fingerprint examination.

Another scenario that is often inaccurately portrayed in many television and film dramas concerns the use of emergency sirens and lights (blues and twos) on police vehicles. In fact the police will only ever activate their emergency sirens and lights on their vehicles when they are en route to an immediate response job. This refers to any incident that involves an immediate threat to the public or their property. In certain situations, such as making oncoming road users aware of a road closure, a police vehicle's lights may remain activated, but the siren will be silenced at the earliest opportunity. Therefore once a scene is secure, it is incorrect to portray other police vehicles appearing hours later or conveying suspects to the police station with lights and sirens blaring, and whilst I appreciate it can add drama to a scenario, it should be avoided.

Cordons at a Crime Scene

One of the most confusing areas for writers is the use of cordons at crime scenes. Cordons are established using police tape, and identify a controlled boundary around the crime scene – the larger the scene, the more the police resources required to monitor it. There are typically two cordons: an outer cordon that keeps the press, public and curious writers at bay, and an inner cordon that secures the actual crime scene and the evidence within it.

Usually the outer cordon will cover quite a large area as it can always be reduced at a later date, particularly when investigators are satisfied that no evidence will be compromised by reducing it. Once a cordon is reduced or released, potential evidence could be lost. A cordon will remain in place for as long as investigators consider it necessary; this time span can range from hours, to days and even weeks, depending on the severity of the incident and the amount of potential evidence within the scene.

A common approach path is usually also set up within the inner cordon, particularly if there is a body in situ. This path is the route that is *least* likely to have been taken by the victim or suspect, and is usually marked out with additional crime scene tape or stepping plates. The purpose of using a common approach path is to prevent investigators trampling over evidence potentially discarded by the victim or suspect.

Police tape secures the outer cordon.

As you can see from the photograph, the police crime-scene tape is glaringly obvious, but it is surprising how many people become 'tape blind'. I have worked on numerous crime scenes where members of the public have asked or even demanded to be let through so they can post a letter, visit a friend, take a shortcut, or quite brazenly just have a good look at what is going on. For whatever reason, although some members of the public see the police tape, they genuinely seem to think that it doesn't apply to them, and seem to consider death and an ongoing murder investigation as nothing more than an inconvenience.

The outer cordon is policed to ensure that nobody enters without permission. As a writer, you may need your characters to see or hear something happening within the cordon if it is relevant to the storyline. However, rather than having your character enter the cordoned area, which just would not be allowed to happen, consider reducing its size so that relevant information can be seen or heard.

Bodies within Cordons

If a body is discovered outdoors, a crime scene tent is used to cover it from prying eyes and to ensure it is protected from adverse weather conditions whilst it is examined before it is taken to the mortuary. It is quite common for a Home Office pathologist (or the coroner's officer if the death is not deemed suspicious – such as obvious suicide) to attend the scene whilst the body is still in situ, so they can establish a clear sequence of events prior to the post-mortem taking place.

The body will be photographed, and tape lifts and swabs taken from any exposed areas of skin to recover any precious trace evidence; it will then be wrapped in a body sheet and placed in a body bag, and conveyed to the mortuary by an undertaker with a police escort to ensure that continuity of the body is maintained.

As mentioned previously, officers who control the cordon will take details of any witnesses who may come forwards, and will pass on their details to CID. As a writer, not only do you have the opportunity to introduce witnesses at this point, but also any suspects. It is often said that villains return to the scene of the crime, and this can be quite true – officers monitoring the cordon may notice the same vehicle or individual passing back and forth and observing the crime scene from a distance.

Also consider that a crime scene can comprise of more than just a physical location such as a building, vehicle or an area of land: a person can be classed as a crime scene, whether victim or suspect, and it is equally important that individuals in this case are also appropriately identified, secured and protected. This is done by seizing their clothing and ensuring they do not eat, drink or wash until any appropriate swabs or samples have been taken from them.

The Scene Log
The first officers in attendance at the crime scene will ensure that a scene log is started. Typically this is a hand-written record of

Crime scene tape secures the inner cordon.

anyone entering the crime scene: it notes their arrival and departure time and their reason for attending. The scene log will be maintained throughout the course of the investigation and will conclude with the time and date that the crime scene is released.

If the crime scene is within a property, then it will be relatively easy to secure with the minimum of police resources surrounding the premises to ensure no unauthorized personnel enter the scene. However, if the scene is outside, this can be slightly more problematic, as previously mentioned, because more resources are needed to secure a larger area. Uniformed officers and police community support officers (PCSOs) are used to secure the crime scene to ensure no unauthorized personnel enter, and also to take details of any potential witnesses who may come forwards.

PROTECTING THE CRIME SCENE

Whatever the type of crime scene, it is essential that it is adequately protected to ensure that no evidence is lost or damaged. Access to a crime scene is limited, particularly in the early stages of an investigation, so be sure to avoid the usual writer's mistake of describing a scene that is trampled over by anyone and everyone, as this would simply not be allowed to happen.

Scene Suits and Boots

It is a job requirement for all police officers and crime scene investigators to provide fingerprints and a sample of DNA for elimination purposes. In addition to this, investigators take measures to avoid leaving their own DNA, fingerprints or fibres at the scene by wearing appropriate protective clothing. This consists of the following:

- a white paper scene suit
- a hair net or hood
- face mask
- gloves
- overshoes

Adequate protective clothing prevents investigators from being unnecessarily exposed to bodily fluids, therefore protecting not just their clothing but more importantly their health, in such cases where the victim or suspect may have a contagious disease such as hepatitis.

A CSI wearing
barrier clothing.

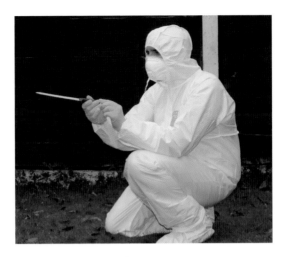

Rank and Files

The majority of crime scenes will not be attended by anyone above the rank of detective inspector. Once a crime scene has been established and appropriately secured, it is then examined in accordance with the strategy devised by the crime scene manager and the SIO. Crime scene investigators regularly update the crime scene manager with their progress, and this is subsequently fed back to the SIO and the investigation team.

At this stage of your storyline ensure that your investigating officer is of realistic rank and is adequately dressed before you allow them access into your scene. Think of yourself as a nightclub doorman: if they haven't got their overshoes on, then they are not allowed in!

The lengths taken to protect a crime scene and the evidence within it depends upon the location and whether it is an indoor or outdoor scene. The worst-case scenario is an outdoor scene with an obvious blood trail and the onset of wet weather. A quick-thinking police officer may be able to cover some of the blood to prevent it being washed away, but it will be nearly impossible to protect the whole trail. It might also be the case that the officer on your crime scene is not so quick thinking and will stand by and watch the rain wash away the evidence under the assumption that the attending crime scene investigator possesses some unknown skill or gadget that will be able to retrieve it.

To use another example, imagine a rape scene situated in a secluded back street in the centre of town. It has been reported that the offender discarded a condom wrapper at the scene, and also a tissue that he used to wipe himself with after the offence. This might seem a relatively straightforward scene to have to examine, but now imagine that it is blowing a gale and the aforementioned evidence is potentially being blown across the town centre. This is a typical example of the trials and tribulations experienced by investigators, and one that you can portray your characters as also experiencing.

Latent Evidence

When examining any crime scene, the consensus is that just because something cannot be seen, it doesn't mean that it isn't there. Not all crime scene clues, such as fingerprints, are visually or immediately obvious. The word 'latent' derives from the Latin word *letere*, which means to 'lie hidden'. 'Latent evidence' refers to evidence that is dormant and requires closer examination or enhancement to identify it. This is summed up by Dr Edmund Locard's exchange principle that 'every contact leaves a trace', described below.

Dr Locard's Exchange Principle

Dr Edmund Locard was born in Saint-Chamond, France, in 1877 and died in 1966. He studied medicine and law, and became a renowned pioneer in forensic science. He is also well known for having set up the first police laboratory for the purpose of examining evidence from crime scenes. Referred to as the Sherlock Holmes of France, Locard summed up the fundamentals of crime scene examination with his theory of exchange:

> Wherever he steps, whatever he touches, whatever he leaves, even unconsciously, will serve as a silent witness against him. Not only his *fingerprints* or his *footprints*, but his hair, the *fibre* from his clothes, the *glass* he breaks, the *tool mark* he leaves, the *paint* he scratches, the *blood* or *semen* he deposits or collects. All of these and more bear mute witness against him.
>
> Dr Edmund Locard, 1877–1966

Because some evidence is latent and therefore not immediately apparent it is essential to avoid contact with surfaces until they have been thoroughly examined, otherwise there is a risk that fragile evidence such as fibres and fingerprints may become rubbed away or damaged.

Whether or not you choose your characters to be aware of this depends on your storyline. Uniformed officers are given some training with regard to crime scene preservation, but if your scene is

Metal stepping plate.

entered by someone who is new, or who forgets their training in the heat of the moment, it is possible that evidence may be destroyed before the scene is even secured. Alternatively it could be that your antagonist has had the forethought to destroy evidence prior to fleeing the scene.

Stepping Plates

Floors tend to contain the majority of evidence within scenes, including blood, footwear marks, cigarette ends and weapons. Each area of the floor is examined before it is walked on, and stepping plates are used to ensure that the floor and any evidence on it are protected.

Stepping plates can be either metal or clear plastic. The benefits of using clear plastic ones are that any evidence under the plate can be seen. However, they have a tendency to slip, particularly on laminate or wooden floors, as they are quite light in weight and not very sturdy.

Metal stepping plates are understandably heavier, sturdier and less prone to cracking, which is useful to know if your characters are a little on the heavy side. Using stepping plates on stairs can be quite precarious, particularly when you consider that investigators are wearing overshoes, which can cause them to slip.

Crime Scene Markers

As crime scene investigators commence their scene examination, they will highlight evidence using either adhesive labels or yellow crime scene markers. This not only highlights the presence of the evidence to others working within the scene, but also allows investigators to demonstrate where each piece of evidence is located in relation to the overall crime scene. This evidence will later be mapped out by a plan drawer.

Numbered markers identify the location of exhibits.

AVOIDING CONTAMINATION

It would be pointless to ensure that a crime scene is correctly preserved if it is then allowed to become contaminated. Referring back to our new car analogy, how would you like somebody to spill food and drink in it, or to smoke in it, potentially leaving a cigarette burn on that beautiful new upholstery? Assuming the answer to this is no, we can consider the effects of contaminating a crime scene and how evidence can become compromised as a result. As a writer, by appreciating the concept of contamination, you will have the opportunity to manipulate a crime scene or a particular piece of evidence to suit your storyline.

As mentioned previously, investigators will not attend a major crime scene until they are dressed adequately in scene suit, mask, gloves and overshoes to protect themselves and their clothing. This also ensures that they do not contaminate the crime scene by depositing their own hair, fibres, DNA and fingerprints within the scene.

Ideally, as few people as possible should enter the crime scene, to avoid the following:

- the risk of contamination
- the risk of damaging fragile evidence
- overcrowding. Space within the scene is usually limited, particularly when using stepping plates

Contamination may occur if evidence is not collected according to correct procedures, or if it becomes accidentally mixed up with other items. It can also occur if the evidence is damaged; for example, a heavy-footed investigator may stumble off a stepping plate scuffing a footwear mark, or grinding fragile evidence into the ground. In order to ensure errors that like this are avoided, crime scene investigators work methodically and at a measured pace.

If a writer were to attempt to detail each and every painstaking step of the crime scene investigation process, I can guarantee that readers will quickly lose interest, switch off and not even contemplate picking up your novel. Therefore, I would advise not committing to the time it takes your characters to conduct a scene examination, unless it is relevant to the storyline. And if it is relevant, bear in mind that as evidence is collected it can be recovered and processed whilst the scene examination continues.

Contamination can also occur if an object from outside the scene is accidentally introduced. Consider the earlier example of the condom wrapper and the tissue: not only can evidence be lost from an outdoor scene on a windy day, but the same weather conditions can cause unrelated items to be blown into the scene, so by the time a crime scene investigator arrives at the rape scene there may potentially be a number of tissues and condom wrappers to be collected.

To avoid unnecessary items being left at a scene, investigators will observe strict policies, such as no eating or drinking within the confines of a scene – although realistically, a decomposing cadaver in situ is usually enough to dissuade investigators from taking food into the scene with them, quite apart from the fact it is completely against procedure.

Be aware that it is not just within the scene that contamination of evidence may occur. Once the evidence is collected, signed, sealed and packaged, it is then sent on to a variety of different sources, such as a local forensic services provider for DNA analysis. There are a number of stringent measures put in place that must be adhered to, so that damage and contamination does not occur to evidence once it is received within the laboratory.

Cross Contamination

Also known as secondary transfer, cross contamination basically occurs when an individual potentially carries evidence from one crime scene to another. In order to avoid this, police officers and crime scene investigators who attend a crime scene (remembering that this can be a physical location or person) will not then attend or deal with additional scenes or suspects.

Once again this allows a writer to manipulate a situation to suit their storyline; for example, a keen-eyed defence barrister might notice the same police officer's collar number cropping up on two scene logs on the same day. The following case study looks at how cross contamination could impact on an investigation, and how easily, without due thought, it could occur.

Case Study: Secondary Transfer

PC Archer and a number of his colleagues respond to the report of an assault, and head immediately to the stated location. On arrival at the scene they find a male lying in the middle of the road, collapsed and bleeding. PC Archer's colleagues begin to disperse the crowd, including suspects and witnesses, as Archer himself concentrates on tending to the victim prior to the arrival of a paramedic.

Once the victim is en route to hospital, Archer goes to liaise with his colleagues, who inform him that a number of arrests have been made. Archer decides to convey one of the arrestees back to the station in his police van. On arrival at the custody suite, he escorts the suspect by the arm to the custody desk.

The suspect later has his clothing seized as part of the investigation. He denies any involvement in the assault, but forensic analysis of his clothing reveals traces of the victim's blood on the sleeve. But has this blood appeared on the suspect's clothing due to his involvement in the assault, or has it been transferred from contact with PC Archer? Without additional evidence, witness statements or CCTV footage it is possible that a guilty man walks free because of cross-contamination issues.

EVIDENCE RECOVERY

Regardless of the evidence type recovered by a crime scene investigator, each exhibit is recorded, exhibited and packaged at the scene. Each and every aspect of a major crime scene is photographically recorded and videoed. In some forces the crime scene investigator will do both jobs, however, in larger forces the CSIs are supported by a specialist imaging unit who will carry out photographic support (for example, at post mortems) and also video crime scenes, and will subsequently produce video evidence that can be suitably prepared and adapted for court purposes.

One of the reasons why crime scenes can seem lengthy and protracted – particularly for local people trying to go about their daily business and wanting to use certain shops, for example – is because each piece of evidence is meticulously recorded and recovered at each stage. Once the scene is secured and the initial scene photographs/videos have been conducted, the crime scene investigator will proceed to recover their exhibits, which are recorded as their initials and a sequential number.

For example, my first exhibit will always be 'KB1 – album of scene photographs'. This may be exhibit 1 of potentially hundreds, depending on the size of the scene and the length of time that I, personally, am there. Also remember that this may be one scene of potentially more than a dozen related to this particular case. My next exhibit may be 'KB2 – blood-stained knife from floor in hall' – and so on.

At each stage of evidence recovery the crime scene investigator will photographically record the evidence, detail it on their job sheet, recover and package it, and then write out an appropriate exhibit label or exhibit bag. It is true to say that in the majority

WRITE USING BALL POINT PEN

Police Force:

Exhibit Ref. No:

Property Ref. No:

Rv _____

Description

Time & Date Found / Seized / Produced:-

Where Found / Seized / Produced:-

Found / Seized / Produced by:

Signed:

Incident / Crime No.:

Laboratory Ref.:

Continuity

Received by Name / Rank / No. (Block Letters)

Signed _____
Time & Date _____

Received by Name / Rank / No. (Block Letters)

Signed _____
Time & Date _____

Received by Name / Rank / No. (Block Letters)

Signed _____
Time & Date _____

Received by Name / Rank / No. (Block Letters)

Signed _____
Time & Date _____

Received by Name / Rank / No. (Block Letters)

Signed _____
Time & Date _____

Received by Name / Rank / No. (Block Letters)

Signed _____
Time & Date _____

Criminal Justice Act (CJA) labels.

of cases, writing up exhibits takes longer than the actual recovery – that is, swabbing a blood stain or packaging a knife. Using packaging tape whilst wearing gloves is also a very frustrating process!

Throughout the course of the scene examination, the crime scene investigator will maintain full and contemporaneous notes detailing their scene examination, from their initial observation, the date and the start and finish times, and a record of the exhibits they have recovered. These notes are a part of the investigation and are admissible in court, as well as being a valuable aide memoire for the crime scene investigator once they are asked to produce a statement, prepare a legend (list) of the photographic albums they have provided, or when giving evidence.

Any evidence recovered from a crime scene will be scrutinized in court by the defence, which is why procedures are put in place to record, preserve and recover relevant exhibits correctly. This includes monitoring the timeline of exhibits. Whenever an exhibit is passed on to the next person or submitted for examination, the person receiving it will sign the yellow exhibit label (or subsequent packaging) known as a Criminal Justice Act (CJA) label. Therefore consider that if you allow your characters to find and remove relevant evidence from a crime scene, its integrity will be compromised and this will negate its value in court.

Communication is an essential part of an investigation, so rest assured that whatever your protagonist needs to discover within the scene will be located by the crime scene investigator and this information will be passed on; your storyline can therefore continue to flow, and your protagonist does not need to be hampered by the laborious, time-consuming scene examination process.

FROM CRIME SCENE TO MOVIE SCENE

Creating fictional crime scenes is nothing new. Frances Glessner Lee, who is also known as the 'mother of forensic science', initiated the teaching of how to examine crime scenes after founding the Department of Legal Medicine at Harvard. During the 1940s and 1950s she created intricate, real life, miniature doll's house crime scenes that were based on real murders, so she could train detectives as to the visual evidence they needed to consider when attending a crime scene.

The models were built with such accuracy and precision that they even included blood splatter, and the angle of the dolls' bodies exactly replicated the position in which they would be found dependent upon the cause of death. Lee's work is entitled the *Nutshell Studies of Unexplained Deaths*, and photographs of the dioramas can be seen in a book by Corinne May Botz. Lee was the first woman to join the International Association of Chiefs of Police in 1943, after she was appointed as captain in the New Hampshire Police.

Whatever type of crime scene your plot includes, you can guarantee it remains plausible by considering the procedures described in this chapter. By ensuring that your character's actions adhere to correct crime scene preservation, such as all personnel entering the crime scene in suitable protective clothing, your writing will portray an element of experience and professionalism. Whether it is a novel or a script you are working on, this accuracy will complement your writing.

Don't feel obliged to write in overly technical detail: just a subtle indication of correct procedure can give your reader a taste of realism. Start to watch or read other crime dramas, and see if you can pick out where writers have correctly or incorrectly used forensic knowledge in their writing – can you now see where poor preservation would realistically compromise a crime scene?

There are also a great many good police documentaries that give an insight into modern day policing, and policy and procedures, such as *The Force*, *24 Hours in Police Custody* and *999 What's Your Emergency?* ITV produced a documentary on the Sadie Hartley murder featuring real footage from Lancashire Police, and this gives invaluable insight into how a murder is investigated from start to finish.

Writing is a competitive industry, so give yourself the chance to succeed and rise above your competitors by being accurate. Allow yourself to produce a compelling piece of writing that is so well researched and authentic that readers don't use your novel as an example of what not to do.

CHAPTER 4

Fingerprints

Fingerprints are undoubtedly the most obvious evidence type to be considered when examining any type of crime scene. Fingerprints are developed in the womb from as early as thirteen weeks, and are fully formed by six months. Pressure is created in the womb due to the position and movement of the foetus, and the density and swirling motion of the amniotic fluid. This pressure is responsible for causing the development of friction ridges and furrows. These ridges and furrows create the thin lines that can be seen on hands and feet (plantar), resulting in the formation of fingerprint patterns; 95 per cent of the skin is smooth compared to the 5 per cent that comprises these ridges and furrows.

One of the earlier pioneers of fingerprints was William Herschel, who recognized the individuality of fingerprints and began privately examining them whilst working in India in 1858. Meanwhile in Tokyo, physician and scientist Henry Faulds had discovered ancient pottery that had been marked with finger and thumb prints. His investigation of these marks led him to realize that fingerprints could be enhanced by using powder.

Faulds discussed his new-found method of retrieving fingerprints, and the possibility of using fingerprint evidence as a means of criminal identification, with the naturalist Charles Darwin. Darwin was intrigued by the idea, and enlisted the opinion and expertise of the anthropologist Francis Galton, who went on to classify eight categories of fingerprint pattern. These patterns, which are also known as Galton's definitions, are still prevalent today.

By the early 1900s a fingerprint classification system had been developed that enabled fingerprints to be collected and stored. This captured the public's imagination as an indisputable method of identifying criminals. Even the fictional detective Sherlock Holmes first considered fingerprint evidence in Arthur Conan Doyle's second Holmes novel *The Sign of the Four* (1890).

Fingerprint Patterns

The pressure of contact in the womb is understandably inimitable, which results in the unique configuration of ridge detail. This means

Fingerprint patterns and classifications.

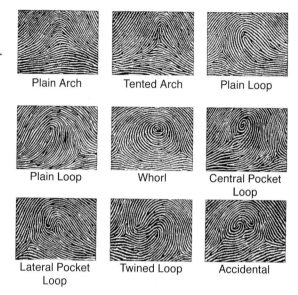

Plain Arch	Tented Arch	Plain Loop
Plain Loop	Whorl	Central Pocket Loop
Lateral Pocket Loop	Twined Loop	Accidental

that each person's finger-prints are unique, even identical twins. Finger-prints are categorized into three main pattern types, namely loop, whorl and arch. Galton further categorized them into eight classifications.

The three main fingerprint patterns.

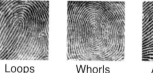

Loops   Whorls   Arches

DEPOSITING FINGERPRINTS

Each fingerprint ridge has pores that allow the secretion of sweat, subsequently resulting in a fingerprint impression being deposited upon certain surfaces when touched. Sweat is a combination of water, acids, oils and protein. Some people are better fingerprint donors than others, depending on how their pores secrete.

Take a look at your own fingerprints. Are you able to identify which type of fingerprint pattern you have? Try pressing your fingers against a smooth, shiny surface such as a glass, mirror, or the shiny underside of a DVD. What type of fingerprint impression has been left? Is it strong and clear, or is it faint and difficult to see? This all depends on the type of fingerprint donor you are, how your pores secrete, and whether your hands are clean, dry or dirty.

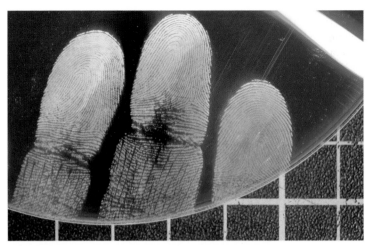

Fingerprints on a DVD.

If you have recently washed and dried your hands they will now be relatively free of oil and might only leave a faint impression – but if your hands are warmer than normal or greasier due to having eaten, the fingerprint mark will be easier to see. However, if your hands are particularly greasy or dirty, the delicate lines of ridge detail become clogged and smudged, and the mark may become too congested, making it difficult to identify.

Now think about what your character is doing when they deposit *their* fingerprints in your crime scene. The chances are that if they are committing a criminal act they might be in a state of agitation or aggression, and consequently their hands are likely to be sweaty or clammy. Their hands might also be contaminated with blood, dirt, accelerants or paint, depending on the type of crime they are committing.

The concentration of contaminant on the hands and fingers may influence the quality of the fingerprint evidence left at the scene. For example, if the hands are too wet this may impair the quality of fingerprints deposited at a crime scene: the mark will become too smeared, and the delicate ridge detail will appear streaked and blurred. Equally if the hands are too dry, this may also result in a poor quality fingerprint, too faint to enhance with conventional fingerprint powders.

Issues Affecting Fingerprint Quality
Skin is made up of two layers – the epidermis is the outer layer and

the dermis is the under layer; the dermis contains blood vessels, hair follicles, nerve endings and sweat glands. Each ridge displayed on the epidermis layer is anchored by two ridges to the dermis layer. In 1934 the infamous US gangster John Dillinger attempted to use acid to burn away his fingerprints – but once the damage had healed, the ridge detail began to grow back.

In addition to Dillinger's efforts, the legendary Ma Barker's youngest son Fred and his criminal counterpart Alvin Karpis also attempted to have their fingerprints removed whilst on the run from the FBI. Joseph Moran was the physician hired to do this, and proceeded to cut away the fingerprints, only stopping when the two criminals could no longer stand the pain. Yet again this attempt was unsuccessful and the ridge detail eventually grew back, because in both cases the damage to the dermis layer had not been deep enough to cause permanent alteration.

Without going to the above extremes, it is possible for individuals to unintentionally cause temporary damage to their fingerprints. There are various factors to consider that could affect the quality of an individual's fingerprints depending on their age, health and even occupation.

Someone employed in manual labour such as a bricklayer or a joiner is likely to wear down the ridges on their hands and fingers by repeatedly carrying and handling heavy materials. And people who regularly use detergents or similar will find that over time these chemicals will have a detrimental impact upon the epidermis, resulting in damage or alteration to their fingerprint patterns.

Ageing effects the skin as the collagen levels are reduced, causing the skin to become thinner and dryer. If you were to compare a child's fingerprints to those of an elderly person, it is apparent how the lack of elasticity affects the plumpness and clarity of the ridge detail. It is likely that the elderly person's fingerprints are crisscrossed with scarring, seen as thin lines.

Arthritis will also influence how an individual donates fingerprints, as the restricted movement in their hands will affect the way they handle objects or surfaces. I have attended crime scenes where it has not been possible to obtain elimination fingerprints from elderly home owners as arthritis has restricted their ability to stretch their fingers sufficiently to be inked and printed.

There are two rare genetic disorders that can result in an individual not forming fingerprints: adermatoglyphia, and Naegli-Franceschetti-Jadassohn syndrome (NFJS) and dermatopathia pigmentosa reticularis (DPR).

Adermatoglyphia: This condition causes individuals to have no fingerprints due to the malfunction of a gene linked to protein. This condition is not known to cause any symptoms other than the lack of fingerprints.

Adermatoglyphia is also referred to as the 'immigration delay disease', as lack of fingerprints means that it is impossible for people with this disorder to prove their identity when they wish to cross international borders. This condition has been the focus of a plot line in the BBC drama *Death in Paradise*.

NFJS and DPR: Naegli-Franceschetti-Jadassohn syndrome (NFJS) and dermatopathia pigmentosa reticularis (DPR) are separate conditions but are classed as the same disorder, as both are caused by the same gene mutation. This disorder is also caused by a defect in the keratin protein gene.

Unlike adermatoglyphia, NFJS and DPR sufferers experience a number of other symptoms affecting the sweat glands, skin, hair, teeth and nails. Those affected also have ridge detail missing from their hands and feet so fingerprints cannot be formed.

A number of skin diseases such as eczema can cause temporary damage to fingerprints, as lesions, scarring and blistering can occur. As these conditions affect the epidermis, the marking of an individual's fingerprints is likely to be temporary, and the ridge detail will heal over time and as the condition improves.

CONDITIONS AFFECTING THE TRANSFER AND DEPOSITION OF FINGERPRINTS

It is not uncommon to examine a crime scene and *not* recover fingerprint evidence, for a number of reasons. As discussed, some individuals are better fingerprint donors than others, and the quality of the mark is very important as there needs to be a number of clearly identifiable characteristics visible to enable a successful fingerprint identification.

Another obvious reason is that the offender may be wearing gloves, although this usually depends on the type of crime and how premeditated it is. For example, a burglar or bank robber will most probably be wearing gloves, but someone who becomes involved in a violent assault probably won't be, as this type of offence tends to be more random.

The pressure of contact and the type of surface touched or handled has a huge bearing on whether there is any likelihood of obtaining fingerprint evidence from a crime scene. We can explore this in further detail by considering the deposition factors of fingerprints in two categories – transfer and environmental.

By being mindful of how fingerprints can or can't be deposited on various surfaces and in various conditions, writers can create a realistic storyline or scenario. Therefore careful consideration needs to be given as to where your characters might leave their clues.

Transfer Factors

The term 'transfer' refers to the types of surface that are touched or handled, and in particular those on which an identifiable fingerprint might be deposited. Consider the texture of the surface – rough textures are not suitable for depositing or retaining fingerprints. Consider the size of the surface area: if it is too small, then not enough ridge detail can be left. Also consider the shape and curvature of the item's surface, as this will also have an impact upon how easily marks are deposited. Pressure is also an important factor as this can impact upon the quality of a mark.

Surfaces are categorized as either porous or non-porous, and this determines which type of fingerprint powder or chemical treatment is used to enhance latent ridge detail. When the word porous is applied to a material, it is referring to an item that has pores or holes in its surface that are capable of absorbing fluid or air. Porous items that are typically subject to fingerprint examination in a crime scene include paper, cardboard, untreated wood and plasterboard. Such items usually benefit from chemical treatment to enhance latent marks rather than conventional fingerprint powders.

Non-porous items are typically smooth items made from glass, UPVC or other plastics, china or glazed pottery and metal. Non-porous items do not absorb, and have the appearance of being relatively smooth and shiny. Items such as glossy cardboard boxes or magazines are considered semi-porous as they are capable of absorption but also have the polished texture of a non-porous item.

Depending on whether a surface or item is porous or non-porous affects the type of fingerprint powder that a crime scene inves-

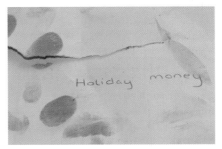

Fingerprints on an envelope enhanced with Magneta flake fingerprint powder.

tigator will choose to use when searching for and enhancing latent marks. Methods of fingerprint examination will be discussed in further detail later on in this chapter. For now we will continue to focus on transfer, and in the following case study will consider the types of surface that are suitable for fingerprint examination and, just as importantly in order to maintain accuracy and realism when writing, which surfaces are unsuitable.

CASE STUDY: EXAMINATION PROCEDURE IN A BURGLARY

In this case study the Laytons' house is the scene of a burglary that occurred in the evening whilst they were at a party. As it had been a hot day they had left the kitchen window open to let in some air. Unfortunately they forgot to shut the window prior to going out, and local burglar and opportunist, Whelan, had spotted this whilst passing by the house.

After checking nobody was in the address, Whelan climbed through the open window, and quickly and quietly searched for any property that had been left lying around. He took a tablet and laptop from the sofa in the lounge, then made his way upstairs where he switched on the bedroom lights so he could search through drawers and cupboards. He also rifled through various items including handbags and jewellery boxes, pocketing some of the more expensive-looking items. He made his way back downstairs where he spotted the family car keys on the hall table. He let himself out of the front door and drove off, with his loot in the stolen vehicle.

We will now consider the types of surface Whelan handled, and ascertain which of these are suitable for a fingerprint examination. The first and most important area of interest to the attending crime scene investigator would be the point of entry window. As the UPVC window frame and glass is smooth, clean and dry, this is a good place to start. From a crime scene investigator's perspective, a non-porous, large surface area that the offender has had to grasp firmly is a good source for fingerprint and footwear recovery. If the area is wet or dirty, however, this makes it a difficult examination, as the investigator will be unable to examine the surface using fingerprint powders.

An initial fingerprint examination at this stage will reveal whether or not the offender was wearing gloves, although it has been known for offenders to remove gloves when opening tricky items such as a cash tin with a tight lid or an envelope that they suspect may contain cash. It is much easier to handle items like this without wearing cumbersome woollen or leather gloves.

An experienced crime scene investigator will usually be able to ascertain the type of gloves worn from the fabric pattern left behind. In some cases, if the pattern of the glove is such that it could be comparable, the glove mark will be enhanced in the same way as a fingerprint and recovered for comparison purposes. This can be useful if the offender's glove is recovered, as the glove marks can be compared – although not an exact science like fingerprint identification, this can provide good intelligence.

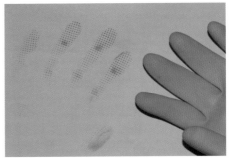

Glove marks can be recovered from a crime scene and compared to a suspect's gloves.

Gloves can also be a good source of DNA, so it is worth remembering that even though your characters might be forensically aware, this doesn't make them infallible

Other surfaces suitable for fingerprint examination include the various boxes that the burglar has rifled through. If these surfaces are not too textured and appear smooth and clean, they are suitable items to be dusted for prints. The crime scene investigator may even consider that boxes that have been ripped open would be better submitted to the forensic laboratory for chemical treatment.

Now we need to consider where else Whelan has been, and which surfaces are *not* suitable for a fingerprint examination. Burglary scenes can look awful: drawers and cupboards pulled open, and clothes and various other items strewn about, bedding disturbed, belongings upended and tossed aside whilst the burglar hastily searches for items of value, without caring about the mess or damage they cause. It isn't their property they are damaging, and they will usually be in a rush so they can get back out without being caught.

Despite the chaotic scene they are faced with, crime scene investigators are limited as to the items and areas they can consider, as many are not suitable for examination. Take, for example, the sofa from where the laptop was taken: fingerprints can't be taken from fabric or leather, so the sofa does not need to be subject to a fingerprint examination – and in reality Whelan would have just picked

A fingerprint coated in aluminium and deposited on a light switch.

up the laptop, rather than touching the sitting area itself. Likewise, any clothing or cloth/leather bags, purses, wallets or briefcases that have been strewn around are not suitable for examination.

Next we might consider the bedroom light switch, and the likelihood of obtaining fingerprints from its surface. But even if Whelan was not wearing gloves, the switch he touched has also been touched numerous times beforehand by the occupants – and it is a relatively small surface area compared to the point-of-entry kitchen window.

In the image above, the fingerprint was left by coating a finger in aluminium fingerprint powder and pressing the light switch, and it clearly illustrates how small the surface area of the light switch is in comparison to a finger tip. Imagine how quickly the light switch becomes congested if touched a second, third and fourth time.

The same rules apply when considering handles. The limited surface area and curvature of these items, not to mention the fact they would have been touched several times, makes them a poor source of fingerprints. These types of item only need touching a couple of times and fingerprints will start to overlap, and the sweat from hands will continue to build up over time. Look at the handles and switches in your own home, and think about how often you touch them. Consider using a (washable) inkpad to see how your prints can be deposited on various surfaces, and see how the marks can build up, slip and overlap.

Now let us consider the stolen motor vehicle. When the police receive information that a vehicle has been stolen the vehicle details are updated on the Police National Computer (PNC). Automated number-plate recognition (ANPR) cameras are used in some police vehicles, and are also placed at fixed locations. This technology is capable of reading registration plates and checking them against a database that will flag up any outstanding stolen vehicles, or vehicles believed to have been used in crime, or that are being driven by a person of interest to the police.

Once an outstanding motor vehicle is recovered, this will usually also be subject to a crime scene examination. The types of surface typically suitable for fingerprint examination include the windows, doors and door frames. Areas such as the glove box, steering wheel, handbrake and gearstick tend not to be suitable for a number of reasons. As previously mentioned, these surfaces are handled so many times they become a mass of overlapped, streaky marks. In addition, the majority of vehicle manufacturers ensure that these areas are designed to maintain the vehicle's clean appearance, so the texture of the surfaces is such that fingerprints cannot be deposited, as the delicate ridge detail of the skin will not adhere to such a heavy substrate.

Be aware, however, that your character may leave fingerprints on items inside the vehicle, such as CD cases, drinks' bottles and paperwork. Trace evidence and DNA may also be recovered from the vehicle. For example, a deployed airbag is potentially a good source of DNA.

Elimination Fingerprints

If fingerprint evidence is recovered, then the crime scene investigator will take elimination fingerprints from the homeowners so that their fingerprints can be compared against the recovered marks. Elimination prints are used purely for elimination purposes and are not stored on any fingerprint database. Once the elimination prints are compared to the scene mark, they are destroyed. Elimination fingerprint forms are also known as 'tenprint' forms.

To avoid the fingerprint database becoming too 'crowded' it is essential that elimination fingerprints are taken, otherwise the scene mark will remain on the database. Fingerprints can be taken by using a pre-inked strip or an ink pad, or an ink block. The ink is applied to the donor's right thumb first, and then over subsequent fingers. The digit is rolled smoothly from left to right in each of the relevant boxes detailed on the elimination form. The plain impressions of all four fingers are taken in a separate box at the bottom of the form, and likewise with the thumbs. There is space available on the reverse of the form to take palm prints.

The donor will be asked to sign the form to record their consent, and confirm that they have been informed that their fingerprints will be destroyed after elimination has taken place.

This is not the only purpose for which fingerprints are taken from innocent members of the public: they may also be taken for emigration, immigration or security clearance purposes. All police officers and frontline police staff such as crime scene investigators and PCSOs are also required to provide elimination fingerprints at the start of their service. As with other elimination prints, these are also destroyed once an employee leaves the police force.

Environmental Factors
Now we have considered the method of transfer involved in depositing good fingerprints within a crime scene, we need to think about

FORM 1154   RESTRICTED

NATIONAL ELIMINATION FINGERPRINT FORM

To be used for the taking of prints from the **victims of crime** and those with **legitimate access** to the crime scene and for **Criminal Record Bureau** appeals purposes.
This form must be completed in BLOCK LETTERS using black ink.
Palm prints should be taken overleaf.   *Bureau Use

CRIME REFERENCE NUMBER

Docket Number*	Taken by: Name		Rank / Number
Fingerprints of: Name	Force (Stn. Code)	Date of offence	D D M M Y Y Y Y
Address	Offence	Place of offence (Stn. Code)	
	SOC Address / Index no. of vehicle		

| Date prints taken | D D M M Y Y Y | Relationship at scene | |

I consent to my fingerprints being taken for elimination purposes. I understand that they will be destroyed at the end of the case and that my fingerprints will only be compared to the fingerprints will only be compared to the fingerprints from this enquiry.

DONOR'S SIGNATURE

1. RIGHT THUMB	2. RIGHT FORE	3. RIGHT MIDDLE	4. RIGHT RING	5. RIGHT LITTLE
				FOLD
6. LEFT THUMB	7. LEFT FORE	8. LEFT MIDDLE	9. LEFT RING	10. LEFT LITTLE
				FOLD

PLAIN IMPRESSIONS

LEFT HAND Four fingers taken simultaneously	TWO THUMBS Impressions taken simultaneously		RIGHT HAND Four fingers taken simultaneously
	LEFT	RIGHT	

RESTRICTED

Elimination fingerprint form.

the environmental factors that affect the deposition of ridge detail. Such factors include temperature, the presence of moisture and if there is any form of contaminant, such as dust, that will affect how a fingerprint is deposited.

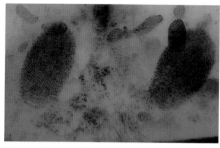

Fingerprints and water marks enhanced with black granular powder.

Fingerprints cannot be recovered from wet surfaces using conventional fingerprint powders, although there are chemical treatments available in the forensic laboratory that are suitable for this purpose. If ridge detail is deposited on a wet surface and fingerprint powders are used to search for marks once the surface has dried, the powder will also enhance water marks, and there is a possibility that this will cause disruption to the mark. The image opposite shows fingerprint marks on the rim of a plate, which have been enhanced using black granular powder. The splodges next to the fingerprints are water marks.

If a finger is pressed against a dusty or gritty surface, this contaminant will adhere to the ridge detail and prevent a positive mark being deposited on the surface. If hands contain a contaminant such as paint or blood, it is possible that the ridge detail will be deposited via the contaminant as opposed to secretion from pores.

If your character, whether they are a suspect or witness, leaves their bloodied fingerprints at a scene, consider the evidential value this has on your storyline, because it may be the victim's blood on their fingerprints, therefore linking them to the scene and the victim. Alternatively, it may be the victim's bloodied prints discovered in the scene – the possibilities for the storyline are endless.

Fingerprints as a Source of DNA
Introducing fingerprints in blood into a crime scene will obviously also allow the possibility for DNA to be included as an evidence type. But how about obtaining DNA from a latent fingerprint mark? The sweat secreted through fingerprints can be forensically analysed using a method known as low copy number DNA (LCN), or a similar method referred to as touch DNA.

These methods only require a small amount of skin cells to be analysed, and they have become a useful tool in re-examining 'cold' cases; however, there are down sides to these methods. The procedures are costly, therefore would only realistically be considered in very serious or high profile cases. Also the process itself and the skin cells analysed are readily subject to cross contamination – that is, DNA from other, innocent individuals – therefore providing a false positive. LCN DNA in particular has been subject to criticism in a number of high profile cases.

Persistence of Fingerprints and Marks

Time is an important factor in most storylines, therefore if the recovery of fingerprint marks is relevant to the plot it is useful to know that there is no scientific method of ageing fingerprint impressions. Depending on the surface they have been deposited on and various environmental factors, fingerprint marks can persist for a long time unless they are physically wiped away. Marks left in contaminants such as paint or putty will also persist until the surface is physically altered.

Not only are fingerprints known for being formed early on in life, they are also one of the few features that remain intact long after death – in fact ridge detail will persist until such time as the flesh on a cadaver reaches the stage of decomposition where the dermis is destroyed. Because each friction ridge is double anchored, such persistence means it is still possible to fingerprint a cadaver even when the skin starts to slip or decay.

If a body curls into the foetal position as a defensive action during, say, an assault or fire, this may help to protect the ridge detail on fingers and palms. Once the body has been subject to a post mortem, a crime scene investigator or fingerprint expert will be tasked with fingerprinting the body, firstly for identification purposes, and to enable the comparison of the victim's marks against any found in the crime scene. Fingerprinting the deceased at this stage will be conducted using the traditional inking method.

In extreme cases where the body is in an advanced stage of decomposition or the skin is damaged due to maceration, charring or desiccation, a fingerprint expert will attempt to recover ridge detail from the deceased using an alternative, appropriate technique. These techniques can include traditional inking and printing, casting, and injecting the digit with water and glycerine (or similar substance) to hydrate and restore the fingerprints. In extreme cases it may even be necessary to remove the hands, but only once permission has been obtained from the coroner, who remains ultimately responsible for the deceased.

Recovering prints from a cadaver is a specialist technique, and one that is not just employed during criminal investigations. In the event of a major incident resulting in mass loss of life, such as the Boxing Day tsunami in 2004, specialists trained in disaster victim identification will recover fingerprints, DNA, dental records and other identifying features from the deceased to assist in identification. In such cases, fingerprints taken from the deceased can be compared to fingerprints recovered from their personal effects found in the home or workplace.

Palm and Plantar Impressions

Although fingerprints have predominantly been referred to throughout this chapter, it is important for writers to consider that ridge detail refers to palm prints as well as plantar impressions. Like fingerprints, palm prints, whether full or partial, are also recovered from crime scenes, and likewise these impressions are taken from victims and suspects.

Plantar impressions are not recorded or stored on any database, but will still be recovered from crime scenes for comparison purposes. Crime scenes where plantar impressions may be particularly prevalent include sexual assault scenes, but they can be useful in other scenarios: I once attended a burglary scene and recovered plantar impressions from a 'quick-thinking' burglar who had removed their footwear before climbing in through a conservatory window. Unfortunately for them their socks were well worn and full of holes, which resulted in them treading areas of ridge detail from their feet over the beautiful, clean, tiled floor. The hapless burglar was disturbed by the house occupants and left to flee in stockinged feet, leaving their trainers behind and a trail of blood because their feet were cut as they ran down the gravel path. The criminal mind is not often the cleverest.

FINGERPRINT IDENTIFICATION

Dactyloscopy, or fingerprint identification as it is better known, is the comparison of fingerprints as a means of criminal identification. Fingerprint experts, who hold a civilian role within the police force, look for specific characteristics and flow within an area of ridge detail, and a cumulative amount of such detail assists in an identification. Fingerprint characteristics, also referred to as minutiae, consist of the following:

- bifurcation
- core
- crossover

- delta
- island
- pore
- ridge ending

crossover
core
bifurcation
ridge ending
island
delta
pore

Ridge characteristics.

Formerly in the UK, fingerprint evidence would only be accepted in court if fingerprint experts were able to confirm that the finger marks in question (the suspect mark and the crime scene mark) had sixteen matching characteristics. In 2001 this was changed in favour of marks being identified through the qualitative rather than quantitative matching of characteristics. In short, the experts are now able to testify that the evidence they have been given sufficiently matches the crime scene mark to the suspect mark, when they can identify an adequate number of unique ridge characteristics and flow.

Identifying an adequate number of characteristics to a specific area of ridge detail allows them to conclude that such uniqueness could only be attributed to that specific individual. When experts make a positive fingerprint identification, it is referred to as an 'ident'.

Ident1 and Live Scan

Once a fingerprint mark has been retrieved from a crime scene and eliminated as being from those people with legitimate access, it is loaded on to the UK's computerized fingerprint database, known as Ident1. A search of the database will result in a number of potential matches with individuals with similar fingerprint patterns to that of the crime scene mark. These matches will then be further examined, and the characteristics searched for and compared by fingerprint experts.

Ident1 has superseded the National Automated Fingerprint Identification System (NAFIS): it has an improved ability to search for palm marks, which NAFIS did not have the automatic capability to do, and it also interacts with another development in fingerprint technology known as 'Live Scan'. Live Scan machines can recover a suspect's finger- and palm prints by electronic means rather than the original method of ink and template. Once prints are recovered

Live Scan machine.

by Live Scan they can be submitted and compared to marks held on Ident1.

FINGERPRINT ENHANCEMENT AND RECOVERY

As mentioned previously, crime scene investigators search for latent fingerprint marks at a crime scene using a variety of fingerprint powders. The powders adhere to the sweat that is secreted through the pores and enhance the ridge detail. The fresher the mark, the easier it is to enhance because the aqueous content of the impression is at its best and therefore the powder will define the mark more effectively.

As the mark ages, the fingerprint powder will work by enhancing the oily secretions that are left, but more build-up of powder may be required to reveal the delicate ridge detail. Crime scene investigators will use either granular or flake fingerprint powder, depending on the type of surface they are examining.

A squirrel-hair fingerprint brush.

Granular Powders

Granular fingerprint powders have been used since the early 1900s and are either black or white. If examined closely they can be seen to contain very small, rounded, grainy particles. The colour of the powder used is chosen according to which will give the best contrast against the background being examined. Granular powders can be used on a variety of surfaces, either porous or non-porous, as long as they are relatively smooth.

Granular powders are applied using animal-hair brushes, usually squirrel hair that may shed occasionally, and if used with too much pressure, damage may be caused to the delicate ridge detail whilst it is being enhanced. The powder is applied lightly, and only built up over the mark where necessary to avoid the mark becoming too clogged up and subsequently damaged. Fingerprints enhanced using granular powders are photographed.

Flake Powders

Flake powders are metallic, typically aluminium or iron, and have been used since the 1970s. Aluminium is a milled, fine powder, silver/grey in colour, and considered to be more sensitive than other powders as it is lighter and less likely to overfill or clog up a mark

Brush loaded with white granular powder.

Aluminium
fingerprint
powder.

than granular or magnetic powders. It is most suitable for use on non-porous surfaces, particularly glass. As with all powders, it should be used in conjunction with a good light source.

Aluminium powder is applied using a glass- or carbon-fibre brush constructed of fine hairs: these shed less and cause minimum damage to the delicate ridge detail of latent fingerprint marks as compared to animal-hair brushes. Typically, crime dramas portray aluminium powder being applied using this brush (also known as a zephyr brush), possibly because it looks quite technical.

Marks enhanced with aluminium powder are recovered using a technique called 'lifting'. This involves using a piece of low-tack adhesive tape of suitable size, or a purpose-made fingerprint lift, which is pressed on to the surface and over the powdered impressions. The tape is then smoothed down on to a clear piece of plastic sheeting such as Cobex. The ends of the tape are then scored, and signed or initialled by the crime scene investigator: this ensures that the tape cannot be removed or the fingerprint lift tampered with without the interference being detected.

Magneta flake powders can be grey or black in colour, and consist of metal and metal oxides that are magnetic. Instead of a brush, these powders are applied using a magnetic wand. When the wand is dipped into the powder it draws the flakes of powder to it, gathering a clump that can then be lightly applied over the surface being examined. By pushing the handle of the wand the magnet is deactivated, and any surplus powder can be emptied back into the pot.

As it is the powder and not the wand that makes contact with any latent ridge detail, it offers greater protection to the mark and causes less damage than powder applied with a brush. This powder is best used on grainy, non-porous surfaces; the fingerprint marks are photographically recovered.

A carbon-fibre brush.

A carbon-fibre brush loaded with aluminium powder.

The Forensic Laboratory

The forensic laboratory is an additional scientific support employed by most police forces, staffed by civilian technicians. The laboratory technicians use various chemical treatments to enhance latent fingerprints, footwear marks, or blood from exhibits or crime scenes. As well as being laboratory based, the technicians will also deploy to major crime scenes to assist in an investigation where additional chemical treatment is required.

Whereas crime scene investigators are restricted to the use of fingerprint powders, the laboratory has access to a plethora of chemical treatments, which can be used sequentially to enhance latent marks from items submitted to them. Amongst the treatments they use are superglue, ninhydrin and a small particle reagent that can be used on certain wet surfaces. In addition to the chemi-

Magneta flake fingerprint powder.

cal treatments available, there is also a wider range of fingerprint powders, including bronze and gold; powders are also available in different colours to allow a wider contrast.

THE BENEFITS OF FINGERPRINTING

Although fingerprints may appear to be superseded by the continued advances in DNA technology, their contribution in fighting crime has been and *will* continue to be invaluable. Fingerprint evidence can be processed much more quickly and cheaply than DNA evidence, and continues to remain superior due to its uniqueness.

The use of fingerprints to assist in identifying the deceased, particularly following the tragedy of a mass disaster, cannot be ignored. In our modern-day society, using fingerprints as a form of biometrics gives Galton's details a fresh lease of life, reminding us just how valuable and useful they are.

EPILOGUE

Cases of interest for further reading include the following:

- Harry Jackson: the first burglar to be convicted based on fingerprint evidence in 1902
- The murders of Thomas and Ann Farrow by the Stratton brothers in 1905
- The murder of Clarence Hiller by Thomas Jennings in 1910
- Shirley McKie and the Strathclyde Police: the Marion Ross murder in 1997

CHAPTER 5

DNA

After fingerprinting, the next biggest development in human identification and its use, particularly in criminal investigations, is deoxyribonucleic acid, or DNA as it is – thankfully – more commonly known. This method of identification, used for paternal and criminal purposes, is now widely recognized by the general public thanks to the *Jeremy Kyle Show* and, more appropriately, the work conducted by the geneticist Sir Alec Jeffreys, who developed genetic fingerprinting and the techniques used for the purpose of DNA profiling.

Whether we are proving our ancestry or attempting to prove guilt or innocence in criminal proceedings, we rely on DNA to be our biological blueprint. DNA is comprised of molecules that carry the particular proteins needed for life to exist, as well as carrying the genetic code that characteristically determines an individual. Unlike fingerprints, it is possible for monozygotic (identical) twins to have the same DNA, because a person's DNA consists of 50 per cent from the mother and 50 per cent from the father.

In 1962, Francis Crick, James Watson and Maurice Wilkins were awarded the Nobel Prize in Medicine for discovering the structure of DNA. Known as the double helix, this is the molecular structure that demonstrates how heredity from DNA is coded and replicated. Pictorially, the double helix looks like a twisted ladder, the steps of which contain four nitrogenous bases that pair together and form a repetitive pattern. The four bases include guanine (G), adenine (A), thymine (T) and cytosine (C).

Guanine is paired with cytosine, and adenine is paired with thymine. Referred to by their initials, these compounds are paired on each step of the double helix ladder and bound together along with deoxyribose sugar and phosphate. This unit is known as a strand, and each nucleotide on one strand is paired with its opposite partner, an arrangement referred to as 'reverse complement sequencing'.

Our individual genetic code is determined by the order of the four bases, in a similar way to how the organization of letters forms a word. Determining the order of these bases into strands is known as DNA sequencing: a basic example can be seen in the image.

```
G ---- A ---- G ---- T ---- C ---- T ---- G ---- C ---- A ---- A
 |     |     |     |     |     |     |     |     |     |
C ---- T ---- C ---- A ---- G ---- A ---- C ---- G ---- T ---- T
```

Reverse complement sequence.

It is the combination of these strands that makes us all unique. DNA is stored within a cellular bundle known as a chromosome, and can be found in every cell that has a nucleus. White blood cells have a nucleus and therefore contain DNA. Gametes are also cells, but are only used for reproduction (sperm and ovum) and therefore do not contain DNA. Red blood cells do not contain DNA either because they have no nucleus.

A blood transfusion comprises predominantly of red blood cells and therefore the donor blood should not genetically impact upon the recipients. In the event that the recipient's DNA profile is altered this change will only last for a few days, which is the time it takes the transfusion to persist.

During an organ transplant, the organ will still contain the donor's cells, which can result in the recipient's cells attacking the alien cells and risking rejection. Drugs can be used to control the rejection and doctors may analyse the recipient's blood for traces of donor DNA to predict and monitor rejection.

In cases where rejection has been managed and the transplant is deemed successful there should only be a miniscule detection of donor DNA. Eventually the cells of the donor organ will be completely replenished with the recipient's cells, therefore eradicating the donor DNA.

THE FORENSIC SCIENCE SERVICE

It would not be possible to write a chapter about DNA without mentioning the Forensic Science Service (FSS). Owned by the Home Office and established in 1991, the main function of the FSS was to provide impartial scientific support and resources to assist investigation into a criminal enquiry. As well as assisting in criminal cases, the FSS also provided assistance to other government agencies such as HM Revenue and Customs and the Crown Prosecution Service.

The FSS provided support, training and guidance to all police forces across England and Wales. At this time all forensic samples seized from crime scenes and which required further scientific analysis were submitted to the FSS. Since its unfortunate closure in March 2012, such samples that cannot be analysed internally within a police force are now submitted to private forensic service providers.

In its lifetime the FSS provided the overwhelming scientific support needed for identifying mass casualties, such as after 9/11 and the 7/7 bombings; it processed and analysed evidence from countless crime scenes, and helped to develop the crime-fighting tools we use today. It also contributed to the development of the hand-held breathalyser, pioneered the use of DNA profiling and developed Low Copy Number DNA, one of the most recent forms of DNA profiling.

If your writing is set in the time period between 1991 and 2012, then the FSS would have been responsible for analysing evidence and providing the scientific support needed at major crime scenes.

THE HISTORY OF DNA PROFILING

Before DNA profiling became available, the FSS and other agencies relied on the method of conventional blood grouping to assist in identification purposes. This method involved analysing blood or other bodily fluids to determine an individual's ABO blood group (either blood type A, B, AB or O), as classified by Jan Jansky in 1907. Alec Jeffreys' groundbreaking discovery led to the first forensic detection in 1987 and the subsequent arrest of rapist and murderer Colin Pitchfork.

Case Study: The Arrest of Colin Pitchfork as a Result of Forensic Detection

On the 21 November 1983, Lynda Mann, a fifteen-year-old schoolgirl, failed to return to her home in Narborough, Leicestershire, after visiting a friend. The following morning her body was discovered – she had been raped and strangled. Using blood grouping, scientists were able to confirm that a semen sample taken from Lynda's body came from a male with type A blood.

On 31 July 1986, Dawn Ashworth, also fifteen, failed to return to her home in nearby Enderby. Her body was found two days later and she, too, had been raped and strangled. A semen sample taken from Dawn also resulted in a match with type A blood.

At the time, police suspected a local teenager with learning difficulties, Richard Buckland, who had knowledge of the murder of Dawn Ashworth. When questioned, Buckland admitted to Dawn's murder, but denied any involvement in the rape and murder of Lynda Mann. Investigators had heard about Alec Jeffreys' success with DNA profiling and asked him to study the two semen samples. Jeffreys concluded that the two samples were from the same man, but that this person was not Richard Buckland, and he was subsequently exonerated, despite his earlier confession. From the samples provided, Jeffreys was able to provide a DNA profile.

With a profile and no other suspects, Leicestershire police asked 5,000 local men to come forward and provide DNA samples, but six months later they were no closer to finding a match. Then in August 1987 a local woman overheard a conversation in a pub, in which a man named Ian Kelly revealed that his colleague, Colin Pitchfork, had paid him £200 to provide a sample in his name. The woman reported this conversation to the police, and Pitchfork was arrested on the 19 September 1987. His DNA profile was conclusive and he was found guilty of the murders, and was sentenced to life imprisonment in 1988.

DNA Profiling Techniques

The DNA profiling developed by Jeffreys is known as the 'multilocus probe technique' (MLP). This method involves cutting the DNA molecules in a chromosome and separating fragments according to their size. This results in a pattern, which has the appearance of a barcode. Although this original method of profiling proved successful, it has its limitations. It required a large amount of biological material to produce a result, and there were problems analysing crime scene stains that had a mix of body fluids. It was also not possible to build a database from the MLP profiles.

In 1990 a more sensitive method of profiling called the 'single locus probe technique' (SLP) replaced MLP. The SLP technique was more suitable for analysing crime scene stains that were damaged or degraded; it could also interpret mixed body fluids such as vaginal fluid and semen. It was possible to store undetected stains on a searchable database, but not SLP profiles.

In 1991 the 'polymerase chain reaction' (PCR) technique was implemented. This is an amplification process that allows the duplication of a DNA sequence until there is a large enough sample to analyse. This means that samples that were previously unsuitable for analysis, such as cigarette ends (a good source of saliva), became suitable sources from which to obtain a DNA profile.

In 1994 short tandem repeat (STR) profiling further developed the PCR technique by copying several areas of the DNA molecule simultaneously. STR has increased sensitivity, allowing further opportunity to obtain profiles from previously unsuitable samples. STR profiles are identified as a sequence of numbers that made it possible to store them on a database, and these were used to construct the National DNA Database in 1995.

STR profiling was followed by five systems, namely Quad, Second Generation Multiplex (SGM), SGM plus, Third Generation Multiplex (TGM) and LCN. These systems were developed in conjunction with STR profiling and looked at copying larger areas of DNA and sex markers to provide a higher discriminating (conclusive) power. The systems allowed profiles to be obtained from more sensitive areas of DNA such as cellular material.

Low copy number (LCN) DNA was developed by the FSS, and has been used since 1999. It copies a greater amount from a smaller sample, meaning a DNA profile can be obtained from a stain the size of a pin head. Because of its sensitivity LCN DNA can easily be contaminated, which is why crime scene investigators and scientists use barrier clothing when collecting and analysing DNA. LCN DNA also requires analysis in sterile, DNA-accredited laboratories, which have strict procedures in place in order to prevent contamination of the sample from the environment it is being profiled in.

Due to its extreme sensitivity, a LCN DNA profile would not necessarily result in the successful identification of an offender, as it is possible that the profile was obtained through secondary transfer from an innocent individual. LCN DNA is a highly sophisticated, invaluable crime-fighting tool, but should only ever be considered as one piece of the investigative jigsaw.

Touch DNA is the newest method of analysis and is an extension of LCN DNA, which involves analysing even fewer skin cells. The risk of cross contamination is still very relevant with touch DNA and, realistically, prolonged contact needs to occur to make it viable. Because such a small number of cells is recovered for analysis it can also make sampling problematic.

If DNA evidence and indeed the method of DNA profiling are going to be relevant to your plot line, be aware of this history of genetic fingerprinting to ensure that you are writing in the correct era to the relevant technique.

Mitochondrial DNA
All the profiling techniques discussed so far relate to the DNA obtained from the nucleus of a cell. Mitochondria are not part of the nucleus, but also exist within the cell and allow the production of energy and respiration. We inherit mitochondrial DNA (mtDNA) from our mothers with no genetic interaction from the paternal line,

which means that siblings and any other relatives linked through the female line will have the same mitochondrial DNA.

There can be hundreds of copies of mitochondrial DNA available within each cell, as compared to a single copy of DNA within the nucleus. These multiple copies are useful in identifying DNA from samples that do not contain a nucleus, such as faeces, hair shafts and bones, and where samples are of a smaller quantity or in an advanced stage of decomposition.

DNA profiles obtained from mitochondrial analysis are not suitable for searching against the DNA database, and are more suited as a tool for personal identification and for tracking ancestry through the maternal line, which can be traced back through hundreds of generations. In 2014, scientists used mitochondrial DNA to confirm that the remains discovered under a car park in Leicester were those of the Plantagenet king, Richard III.

Familial DNA

Familial DNA involves using the genetic information of a relative to help investigators locate a suspect. The DNA database will be searched for family members with a similar genetic match, who will then be interviewed for the purposes of tracing or identifying the nearest possible match. Using familial DNA to identify other DNA profiles allows detectives to create new investigative leads, where previously all other forensic evidence and lines of enquiry have been exhausted.

Familial DNA analysis was first used in a criminal investigation in 2000 in the case of child murderer Joseph Kappen. In 1973, three teenage girls, Sandra Newton, Geraldine Hughes and Pauline Floyd, were raped and strangled, and their bodies dumped in a wooded area near Port Talbot in South Wales. Despite a comprehensive, wide-ranging search no suspects were identified, and Kappen's heinous crimes remained unsolved.

In 2000, a scientist working for the FSS, Dr Whitaker, used familial DNA testing in an attempt to trace the murderer from the crime scene stains deposited back in 1973. Familial DNA testing and Dr Whitaker's logic reasoned that there was every likelihood that in the time since the initial murders, the suspect's siblings or children may have had *their* DNA profile stored on the DNA database.

Sure enough, car thief Paul Kappen was subsequently found to have a DNA profile 50 per cent similar to that of the murderer Joseph Kappen. Unfortunately, detectives discovered that Kappen had died of cancer several years earlier. However, his remains were eventually exhumed and DNA samples were obtained from his remaining teeth and femur, confirming that he was the murderer of the three girls, bringing some relief and closure for their families.

One particular case where familial DNA resulted in the identification of the offender is that of James Lloyd in 2006. It transpired that Lloyd, a seemingly normal family man, pillar of the community and company manager, was actually a prolific, violent sex offender. Between 1983 and 1986, Lloyd stalked and attacked lone women he found walking the streets of South Yorkshire after leaving pubs or clubs. He tied them up with their tights and attacked them before stealing items of jewellery, and also their shoes, which led to him being known as the 'shoe rapist'. But despite extensive police work and many appeals, including one on the BBC programme *Crimewatch*, Lloyd remained undetected.

However, in 2006 his previously unidentified DNA, which had been recovered from the 1980s crime scenes, was eventually linked to him, following his sister's arrest for a drink-driving offence. The DNA sample taken following her arrest was one of a potential forty-three profiles that were found to be similar to Lloyd, following a cold case review and using the method of familial DNA testing.

Police interviewed the sister and arrested Lloyd, who attempted suicide once he found out the police wanted to speak to him. A police search of Lloyd's business premises revealed a trap door, which led to a cache of over 100 pairs of stiletto shoes and other 'trophies'. Lloyd admitted raping four women and attempting to rape a further two, and was sentenced to a minimum of fifteen years' imprisonment.

THE NATIONAL DNA DATABASE

Launched in 1995, the National DNA Database (NDNAD) is the largest in the world: it stores over seven million profiles obtained from unsolved crime scene stains, as well as those taken from individuals arrested and charged with an offence. DNA swabs are taken from individuals typically using a buccal swab. However, a blood sample or a collection of hairs with roots can also be taken, as these are classed as non-intimate samples according to the Police and Criminal Evidence Act 1984.

When a new DNA profile is loaded on to the National DNA Database it automatically searches against any profiles from outstanding crime scene stains, therefore it is possible that the DNA profile of someone arrested on suspicion of burglary matches a profile obtained from a violent robbery scene. If a DNA profile leads to the identification of a suspect, then a further DNA sample will be taken following their arrest. DNA samples may also need to be taken from victims of crime for comparison purposes. A police elimination database also exists, which stores the DNA of serving police officers and civilian police staff, such as crime scene investigators.

When a profile loaded on to the DNA database successfully identifies an individual, this is known as a 'DNA hit' and could potentially establish the following links:

- A scene to person hit – this places an individual's DNA within the crime scene
- A scene to scene hit – this occurs when crime scene stains from different locations have the same profile, therefore making it possible to link those scenes to the same offender
- A person to person hit – this identifies individuals who have given alias details in the past

Since 2012, following the Protection of Freedoms Act, the DNA profile of a suspect who is not charged or is found not guilty is deleted from the database. Prior to this their DNA profile would have been retained indefinitely. However, the DNA profile and fingerprints of an individual who is found guilty of a recordable crime will be retained.

SOURCES OF DNA

Good sources of DNA include blood, tissue, semen, vaginal fluid, mucus, saliva and hair with roots. As a writer, when thinking about which source of DNA is relevant to your storyline, think about where it has been recovered from, and whether it has come from a movable source that could have been planted in your crime scene legitimately or, to add a twist, left purposely to frame someone.

The likelihood of obtaining a DNA profile from blood is over 90 per cent, making it the most valuable source of DNA recovery. The success rate for obtaining a profile from a semen sample is as high as 70 per cent and from saliva it is over 40 per cent. Hair is a good source of DNA, particularly if it still includes the root. Also, because of the propensity for hair to shed, it is also considered a good source of trace evidence (*see* Chapter 7).

When writing, you need to consider if your chosen source of DNA has been discovered in the scene as part of a disturbance, such as blood splatter on walls or hair pulled out during a fight. Or has the DNA been recovered from an item within the scene, such as hair from a hat, or saliva from a drinks container or a piece of

Good sources of DNA.

chewing gum? As a writer, it is much easier fictionally to derive ways of depositing the DNA of a suspect or victim in a crime scene than their fingerprints, as there are more sources and increased opportunities available.

Poor sources of DNA include urine, faeces, menstrual blood and vomit, as these contain poor cellular material. Although it is possible to extract DNA from such samples, it is only possible to extract mitochondrial DNA, so these sources are less desirable than the other sources mentioned. However, when examining major incidents such samples may still be recovered.

BLOOD PATTERN ANALYSIS

Blood pattern analysis (BPA) is a specialist area that concentrates on the examination, identification and interpretation of blood patterns within a crime scene. Although some crime scene investigators may have additional training or experience in how to interpret blood spatter, specialist forensic biologists will be brought in to assist with the examination and interpretation of blood distribution following a serious incident.

Where it is not possible for a scientist to attend a scene, the crime scene investigator will photographically record the scene, paying particular attention to the distribution of blood, using arrow stickers as a gravitational marker and taking close-up photographs of the staining with and without a scale to measure the droplets. This makes it possible for experts to provide an opinion based on the photographic evidence. Blood pattern analysis can be used to interpret staining on the clothing of an assailant as well as at the actual crime scene.

Blood pattern analysis can have a huge impact when presenting evidence in court, as it is an effective way of reconstructing the crime scene and demonstrating the amount of force and violence used during an attack. Analysts will consider a number of factors when analysing a scene, including the texture of the surface of distribution, and the direction and angle of the blood flow. The appearance of the blood staining can also provide a valuable insight into the distribution, as it is influenced by factors including gravity, velocity and viscosity – in other words direction, speed and force.

Analysts have classified a number of specific blood patterns that occur depending on the flight characteristics, and these can be used both to describe and to interpret the distribution. Such classifications include single drops, which are self-explanatory and refer to how blood drops through gravity, from a wound or weapon; this will possibly result in a blood trail or secondary spattering, which occurs when the blood drips on to a surface resulting in further spattering. Evidence of secondary spattering on an individual's clothing, footwear or property is indicative of the fact that they were present at the time of the assault.

'Cast-off' refers to the distribution of blood as it is shed from a bloodied weapon, hand or foot. Cast-off blood staining can appear to be distributed in a straight or curved line dependent on the swing and movement of the blood-stained object. The number of cast-off marks can indicate how many times the victim has been hit. With repeated swinging, less cast-off occurs as blood is shed, unless impact is repeated, in which case a greater quantity of blood will be shed from the backward swing due to heavier blood staining.

The forward swing will produce smaller staining as the quantity of blood diminishes. There can be many variations affecting cast-off, such as the volume of blood and the possibility that multiple weapons, hands or feet were involved; at times this makes it a very difficult pattern to interpret.

Transfer blood stains are also known as contact stains, and these occur when a blood-stained individual or item makes contact with another surface, such as a tap, light switch or door handle, thereby transferring blood on to that item. This transfer also allows the potential opportunity for fingerprint and footwear evidence if fingerprints and footwear marks in blood are discovered on an item or at a crime scene.

Transfer blood staining is beneficial in so much as it allows investigators an opportunity to piece together the series of events following a violent assault. Finding transfer blood stains on surfaces can be indicative of the suspect's movements following the attack.

Arterial stains probably look the most violent, as the viscosity and velocity of pressurized blood pumping from a punctured artery is phenomenal. The arteries that are typically vulnerable as a result of a violent attack or suicide attempt include those situated on the forehead, neck, wrist, heart, thigh and upper arm. The blood pattern arising from this type of injury depends on whether the victim is moving, which artery is damaged and the size of the injury. If there is damage to the throat, the expelled blood may appear diluted due to the presence of saliva or mucus, and the resulting blood pattern may appear to look like a fine mist. Oxygenated blood will appear brighter red in colour.

Blood pooling occurs following prolonged bleeding. If there is no body present it is still possible to establish whether death has occurred due to the volume of blood at the scene. When there is blood pooling present, and indeed any other type of blood pattern, a void may occur, which suggests that an object or individual was present at the time of the incident but has subsequently moved or been moved, a circumstance that is indicated by a stain-free gap within the crime scene.

By recognizing the different types of blood pattern and their potential cause, writers can use this information to describe a crime scene in detail and with better clarity.

Other factors may influence the examination of blood pattern analysis in a crime scene. If alcoholics or drug users occupy the scene location, then there is likely to be a number of sources of blood staining due to needle use, and injuries sustained through falling or fighting. It may also be the case that an attempt has been made to clean the blood away prior to police attendance – though even when blood has been removed with cleaning fluids it is still possible to find traces of it in the crime scene due to the resilience of proteins in the haemoglobin.

SEARCHING FOR BLOOD AND OTHER BODILY FLUIDS

There are certain pieces of equipment that crime scene investigators, laboratory staff and scientists may use when searching for blood and other bodily fluids. These include a good light source, a presumptive blood-testing kit, presumptive tests for semen and saliva, and a forensic drying cabinet.

A Good Light Source

Blood stains can differ in colour depending on the source and age of the blood. Arterial and capillary blood is bright red, whereas venous blood is darker in colour. Think about the colour of the blood you see when you cut yourself, compared to the darker red of the blood you see when providing a blood sample. A fresh blood stain will appear brighter and glossier than an older one, which will appear dull and darker as the protein ages. The appearance of the stain is also influenced by the surface it is deposited on and the surrounding temperature and humidity.

Because of the unclean nature of some crime scenes or even cloth-ing that is subject to examination, it may be difficult to distinguish between blood staining and other similar coloured stains such as food and drink, paint or varnish, rust or faeces. Not all crime scenes look like a blood bath, particularly if they are a secondary scene, such as a suspect's house. In such cases, the crime scene investigator will be searching for transfer blood stains, which may be minute.

A good light source is invaluable when searching for blood, or indeed any latent or trace evidence. An ultraviolet (UV) light can also be useful during a blood search, as it can provide an alterna-tive contrast when searching different coloured surfaces. Under a UV light a body fluid such as semen or saliva will fluoresce very brightly, whereas blood appears black. In addition to the lighting and torches carried by crime scene investigators, laboratory staff may attend a crime scene to assist in the search for bodily fluids, fingerprints or fibres, and they will use a high-intensity light source known as a quasar.

Presumptive Blood-Testing Kit

When a potential blood stain is found at a crime scene, the crime scene investigator will use a presumptive blood-testing kit to ascer-tain if it *is* blood. Types of testing kit available include Hemastix, Kastle Meyer (KM) and Leucomalachite Green (LMG).

Hemastix are typically used to detect traces of blood in a urine sample: they are 3in-long, thin strips of plastic with a small, square yellow pad at one end. The crime scene investigator will take a sterile cotton swab and lightly moisten it in distilled water before rubbing gently at the suspect stain. The swab is then placed against the yellow pad, which will change to dark green if the stain is blood. This occurs because the yellow pad contains a blood-reagent

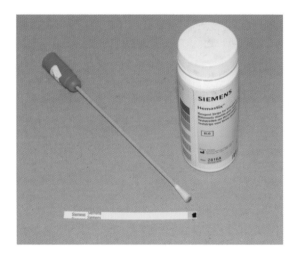

Hemastix indicating a positive result for blood.

material known as tetramethylbenzidine, which reacts to the peroxidase enzyme in haemoglobin.

Kastle Meyer and Leucomalachite Green work in a similar way to Hemastix, and will react to the presence of peroxidase to cause a colour change. Kastle Meyer uses a chemical called phenolphthalein. To use this test, a circular piece of filter paper is folded to make a point, which is then rubbed against the suspected blood stain. The filter paper is unfolded and a drop of the Kastle Meyer is added to the stain, followed by a drop of hydrogen peroxide. If the stain turns pink, this indicates that it is blood. LGM works in the same way as Kastle Meyer, but the resultant colour change is green.

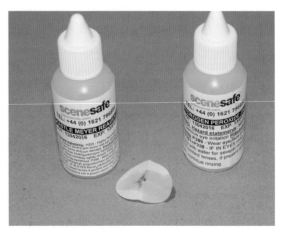

Kastle Meyer: the pink reaction on the filter paper indicates positive for blood.

These kits are referred to as 'presumptive' due to the possibility of their providing a false positive result. Certain chemicals derived from plant organisms, such as horseradish, cleaning solutions and rust, can provide a positive reaction. The testing kits come with a 'use by' date as they can degrade with age, increasing the risk of providing a false positive result.

Presumptive blood-testing kits are not able to distinguish between human and animal blood because all vertebrates have haemoglobin and will therefore produce a positive result. However, scientists can differentiate between human and animal blood by testing for specific proteins, or by looking for a DNA sequence.

With the exception of some primates, a DNA sequence will not be obtained from animal blood. It is possible to ascertain if the blood is human or animal by using a procedure known as the precipitin test, which is conducted by laboratory staff where necessary; however, this is not something that can be done at a crime scene.

Luminol

Of all the presumptive blood-testing kits, luminol, which comes as a manufactured brand such as Blue Star, is the most dramatic. I have seen this used at a few crime scenes and have been impressed every time. It is more commonly used at crime scenes where blood has been cleaned away. With the naked eye the scene appears to be free of blood, but when luminol is applied, blood spatter, contact marks and footwear marks in blood all glow like a fibre-optic Christmas tree.

Luminol works on blood stains that are old, altered or diluted. It is applied as a spray, which, when distributed across an area containing traces of iron from haemoglobin, emits a blue light. However, there are down sides to using this product, because it may provide a false positive – as with the aforementioned presumptive blood tests – due to reaction with other chemicals and even, in some cases, faeces.

Luminol is most effectively viewed in the dark and is therefore applied in a darkened room, which is not without its hazards. Once applied, the results are photographically recorded. This must be done promptly because the luminescent glow only lasts for around thirty seconds. Because luminol is applied as a spray, swabbing the highlighted blood also needs to be done quickly, because if there is only a small drop of blood it can become over diluted and may trickle away.

Luminol has been criticized in the past for causing degradation of the DNA samples obtained following its application. However, research has indicated that it is more likely the presence of hydrogen peroxide that is detrimental to the sample. In addition to this, crime scenes that have been cleaned down using bleach are more likely to be responsible for the degradation of DNA. Either way, it means that all other traces of evidence should be recovered prior to the application of luminol, which is used towards the end of a scene examination.

Presumptive Tests for Semen and Saliva

Presumptive tests are also used on samples assumed to contain traces of semen and saliva, and are carried out by forensic biologists in the laboratory. Crime scene investigators search for semen at scenes where it may be present on clothing, bedding, sanitary towels or condoms. These exhibits are then photographed, exhibited, packaged and submitted directly to the laboratory. If traces of semen are present on a floor or other surface that is not suitable for submission to the laboratory, then it is photographed and swabbed using sterile water and a cotton swab.

On receipt of the exhibits, the biologists rely on a method known as the 'acid phosphatase test'. Acid phosphatase is an enzyme secreted from the prostate gland, and which is subsequently present in seminal fluid. The application of a substance known as alpha-naphthyl phosphate and an additional reagent causes the acid phosphatase to turn purple in colour. This test is successful on seminal fluid that may or may not contain spermatozoa. If it is relevant to your storyline, it is worth considering that semen can persist on certain fabrics for a number of months.

The buccal cells on the inside of the cheeks are the source of DNA in saliva, and it is these buccal cells that are swabbed when taking DNA samples for criminal or hereditary identification. Saliva is also obtained from drinking vessels using the swabbing method, while items such as chewing gum and cigarette ends are submitted to the forensic services provider in the appropriate packaging. As well as being the constituent of spit, saliva may also be recovered from a fresh bite mark, and is also likely to be present following a sexual assault if the offender has licked the victim.

It is the enzyme known as salivary amylase that is present in saliva, and a process known as the Phadebas amylase test is used to detect these traces in a similar way to the acid phosphatase test. As well as being a potentially good source of DNA, saliva is also useful for detecting traces of drugs and other toxins.

The Forensic Drying Cabinet

Where a violent assault has occurred it is accepted that the clothes of the victim or the offender may be heavily bloodstained. As DNA evidence can degrade quickly on wet clothing, the crime scene investigation unit has a forensic drying cabinet. These cabinets are designed to dry out wet evidence from a crime scene in a secure, tamper-resistant, re-circulatory environment that preserves odour and particulates. Each cabinet contains a hose and drain outlet so the crime scene investigator can sterilize it between uses, therefore keeping it free from any potential risk of cross contamination.

Forensic drying cabinet.

THE BENEFITS OF DNA

When reading through the history of DNA profiling, it is astonishing to think how far we have progressed in such a relatively short space of time. Furthermore it is intriguing to think how DNA techniques will continue to progress in the next fifty years, along with their valuable contribution to criminal investigations and genetic and personal identification.

Like any other form of evidence, DNA is not infallible and there are countless opportunities for error, particularly when cross contamination occurs. As a source of evidence, it should never be solely relied upon to bring a conviction, as many other avenues of investigation are required in order to build a strong case.

As a writer, having DNA as a tool provides a great deal of scope when plotting storylines, and the many sources of DNA available allow for the creation of a compelling plot. Knowing how DNA evidence is shed, searched for and collected allows the writer extra confidence when detailing scenes that subsequently add veracity and drama to their storyline.

EPILOGUE

Cases of interest for further reading include the following:

- Execution of the Romanov family (1918) and DNA evidence
- Ronald Castree and Stefan Kiszko – the murder of Lesley Molseed (1975)
- Azaria Chamberlain (Australia, 1980) and the interpretation of forensic evidence
- Simpson and Goldman murder (1994): O. J. Simpson trial and cross-contamination issues
- Damilola Taylor murder (2000) and the use of forensic evidence
- The woman in the suitcase (2002): the murders of Hyo Jung Jin and In Hea Song
- Craig Harman – first conviction using familial DNA (2004)
- Antoni Imiela (M25 rapist) – identified through DNA profiling (2010)

CHAPTER 6

Footwear

If Prince Charming had lived in the twenty-first century he could have found Cinderella in half the time it took him and his palace staff in the fairy tale. If CCTV and automatic number-plate recognition weren't successful in tracking down the pumpkin carriage, then he could always have turned to the forensic clues that she may unwittingly have shed at the scene.

As we now know from previous chapters, our illustrious princess could have been identified through the DNA from her saliva or her fingerprints left on a drinking glass – but what about that infamous glass slipper? Did the prince have forensic awareness concerning the evidential value of her shoe? In this chapter we will look at footwear and how it can be a useful source of evidence, and one which can be attributed, where necessary, to your own protagonists and storylines.

Footwear marks will nearly always be left at a crime scene, unless you create a criminal protagonist who walks on their hands. If suspects or victims are not wearing footwear, there is the potential to recover plantar impressions or sweaty fabric marks deposited as a result of wearing socks or tights. I have also known some 'forensically aware' burglars cover their shoes with carrier bags to prevent leaving footwear impressions on floors or window ledges, but this can be complicated, firstly because of the risk of tripping or slipping, and secondly, because if the carrier bags are disposed of at the scene but subsequently recovered by the crime investigator, they would be a very good source of fingerprints – and the footwear marks on the bags may be enhanced using chemical treatment anyway, so our careful burglar's efforts would be in vain.

Whether a crime is premeditated or spontaneous, in the vast majority of cases, suspects and victims will be wearing some kind of footwear, which will ultimately result in an impression being deposited in a crime scene. But whether our characters resemble Imelda Marcos and have thousands of shoes, or have just one pair, what is it about shoes that make them unique enough to be considered a valuable evidence type?

WHAT MAKES FOOTWEAR UNIQUE?

We have already seen that the uniqueness of fingerprint and DNA evidence makes these a conclusive source of evidence when recovered from a crime scene. But how can we say the same about shoes? What if the fairy godmother manufactured hundreds of thousands of glass slippers in exactly the same way as sports manufacturers such as Nike, Reebok and Adidas do today? How would the prince be able to differentiate between so many Cinderellas with the same shoe size?

Discovering footwear marks at a crime scene enables investigators to establish how the suspects have entered and left the scene. They will also be able to ascertain the minimum number of people who were present and potentially reconstruct their movements within the scene.

There is no set standard of identification required for a footwear expert to be able to conclude that a particular piece of footwear can be matched to a footwear mark recovered from the crime scene. Rather, the evidential value can be determined by the following attributes: size, pattern, degree of wear and corresponding accidental marks.

Size

The size of the shoe is determined by the upper part of the shoe rather than the sole. The sole gives an indication of the length of the wearer's foot, whereas the upper part of the shoe accommodates the foot and so determines the size. Regardless of this, the length of the sole can still be used for comparison purposes, even though it may not necessarily reflect the wearer's shoe size.

The size of the foot may be proportional to a person's height, although this is not an exact science and therefore should only ever be used as an indication. When recovering footwear evidence from a crime scene, it is important to consider whether your character has deliberately worn a pair of shoes that are too large or too small in order to influence the length of sole pattern deposited at the scene. Relevant to this is the case of American anarchist Theodore Kaczynski.

Between 1978 and 1995 Kaczynski conducted a terrorist campaign using homemade bombs, which resulted in the death of three people and the maiming of a further twenty-three. The Federal Bureau of Investigation (FBI) initiated one of their most expensive and protracted investigations in trying to identify and capture the elusive bomber. The case was known as UNABOM, an acronym for Kaczynski's campaign of terror against universities and airlines, which is where he planted the majority of his bombs.

Kaczynski's motivation was fuelled by an abhorrence of modern science and technology, and any businesses that he considered were detrimental to the environment. The 'Unabomber' was highly intelligent and very perceptive, which is why he was able to evade the authorities for as long as he did. He liked to taunt investigators with clues, but he was very forensically aware. On one occasion he found two head hairs at a bus stop and planted them in one of his homemade bombs in an attempt to fool detectives.

Following his arrest, investigators discovered his diaries in which he had recorded all his criminal activity in great detail, even revealing how he had made efforts to disguise any footwear evidence he may have inadvertently left at scenes. He did this by attaching smaller size soles to his shoes, so officers would think their suspect was a shoe size smaller than he actually was.

Kaczynski is currently serving eight life sentences with no chance of parole. But just imagine what such an intelligent, accomplished person could achieve if they set their mindset and passion to achieving non-criminal endeavours.

Pattern

The National Footwear Reference Collection was launched in the United Kingdom in 2009. It characterizes different patterns and styles of footwear from the manufacturers, and produces pattern

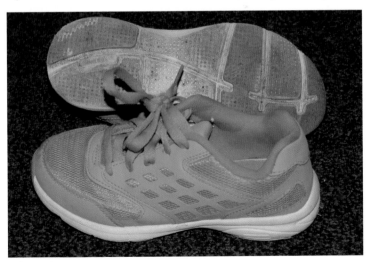

Soles and uppers.

coding, which is then used as a reference source for comparing and matching sole patterns retrieved from crime scenes. Computerized technology such as the Shoeprint Image Capture and Retrieval Version 6 (SICAR6) can interface with footwear reference databases such as SoleMate, which is updated several times a year with details of the latest patterns and brands.

Identifying which type of brand a sole pattern has originated from is one of the earliest stages of comparing scene marks to a suspect's shoes. If the shoe pattern and scene mark pattern don't match, then no further examination is needed. However, if they do, then this is the starting point of the investigation. The discovery of footwear patterns may mean that investigators can link crime scenes together, particularly when the same footwear pattern is recovered from a scene with a similar MO, such as those recovered from linked series burglary scenes.

The upper part of the shoe, particularly when it comes to trainers, can be very distinctive, and it is useful for investigators to have a way of tracing particular brands by their style. Being able to identify the particular brand of a shoe, boot or trainer can be useful when an investigation relies on CCTV images, which has captured a suspect or victim who may only be identifiable through his distinctive footwear.

When considering the pattern, footwear experts will also take into consideration the particular mould of the shoe. Under-soles are typically manufactured either by pouring or injecting the foam that will form the sole into a mould, or by cutting the sole out of a piece of pre-moulded rubber. The cutting method allows for greater variation in the end product because of the way the cutting operator works.

The moulding process also allows for variation due to the inherent difference (however slight) of moulds, even those that produce the same pattern – even a hairline crack or similar feature in the mould will be reproduced in the finished product. Therefore, if a footwear specialist can establish that a piece of footwear and a crime scene footwear mark are the same pattern *and* produced from the same mould, this will strengthen the evidential value of the piece of footwear.

Degree of Wear

Throughout this chapter we will be looking at the way crime scene investigators search for and recover footwear marks from crime scenes, and how this information can add weight to an investigation. However, when considering the degree of wear, we are going to look at the methods used by footwear specialists to physically place suspects into particular shoes. It may be possible to obtain a DNA profile from well-worn shoes, but this can be problematic if several people have worn the shoes, therefore resulting in mixed DNA profiles.

Alternatively, DNA could be found on shoes, which links the suspect to the scene of the crime. If the soles of the shoes are found to bear traces of the victim's blood, this would indisputably place them in the crime scene, and a biologist's interpretation of blood splatter on the shoes could put the wearer in the scene during the victim's attack. Their interpretation can conclude whether the suspect was kicking or stamping the victim, or if they were present during the assault or stabbing, depending on the direction of the blood pattern.

A footwear specialist can conclusively identify an individual as the wearer of a particular pair of shoes, using an appropriately named technique called 'Cinderella analysis', which works on the basis that everybody's feet are different. The features of the foot that make it unique include the ridge characteristics, its morphology – which refers to the shape and form of the foot – and the biomechanical function, which relates to how the foot moves.

In the majority of cases, most of us are likely to have one foot that is slightly larger than the other. The foot characteristics that the specialist will look at in order to establish if the suspect is the wearer include the following:

- the length, width and shape of the foot
- the characteristics on the side of the foot
- the shape and placement of the toes
- the tension points on the upper and under surfaces of the foot
- the pressure points of the tips of the toe

The aim of Cinderella analysis is to prove that an individual can be matched to the particular wear in the shoe. The best way for me to demonstrate how unique this can be is to suggest you try on somebody else's shoes that are quite well worn and the same size as your own – or try putting your own shoes on the wrong feet. This should allow you to observe how the curve of your foot differs from the wear of the shoe – how, for example, the arch and pressure of *your* foot causes it to lean differently in the shoe than is indicated by the well-worn groove left by the original owner.

Now that we know how we can place a suspect into a particular pair of shoes, we need to see how those shoes leave their unique impression at a crime scene.

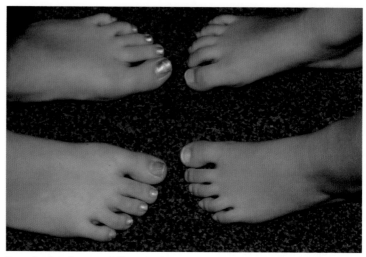

Everybody's feet are different.

Corresponding Accidental Marks

The older the shoe, the greater the chance there is of the sole developing wear and tear due to its repeated impact with the ground. A burglar will repeatedly walk over smashed glass or pieces of splintered wood from doors they have kicked in, and such randomly acquired marks are what makes each individual piece of footwear

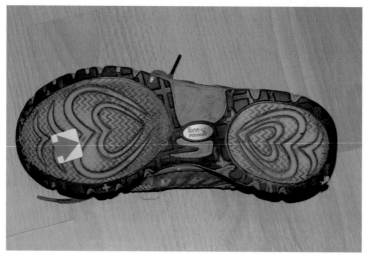

The arrow indicates wear and accidental damage to the sole.

unique. These marks are therefore of strongest evidential value when the piece of footwear is compared with the sole marks at a crime scene.

The evidential value of such marks can, however, become aged due to the continued scarring of well-worn soles; crime scene marks are realistically only evidentially valuable for six months. After this time it is considered that further accidental damage will cause the sole to become considerably more altered, even resulting in previous damage disappearing as the sole wears down.

Comparison of a crime scene mark to a suspect's footwear is carried out by making an imprint of the suspect's shoe on a piece of plain paper. This 'test' mark will be enhanced using magnetic fingerprint powder or similar, and then the footwear specialist can begin comparing size, pattern and corresponding accidental marks.

Footwear mark enhanced with magnetic fingerprint powder.

ELIMINATION FOOTWEAR MARKS AND SUSPECT SAMPLES

When fingerprints and DNA are recovered from the crime scene, investigators need to differentiate between the suspects and those with legitimate access by obtaining elimination samples. The same considerations apply when footwear evidence is recovered from a crime scene.

If the murder scene has been trampled over by paramedics and police officers then this may result in multiple footwear marks in blood. As it is not practical to seize their shoes, elimination prints can be taken using a purpose-made inkless pad and paper, such as the brand known as Printscan. It may also be necessary to take elimination prints from the victim's shoes so the footwear specialist can interpret movement within the scene.

If someone is arrested on suspicion of burglary offences and/or sexual or violent assaults, then officers can seize their footwear so comparison can be made to crime scene marks, as governed by the Police and Criminal Evidence Act (PACE) 1984. The Serious Organised Crime and Police Act (SOCA) 2005 also allows investigators to obtain overt impressions of footwear for intelligence purposes.

GAIT ANALYSIS

It is not just footwear evidence that can be useful in a criminal investigation: even the way the suspect walks can incriminate them. This fact was especially relevant in the case of John Saunders, who in July 2000 was convicted at the Old Bailey for a series of robbery and firearms offences. Saunders was the leader of a gang who orchestrated a series of robberies on jewellers in Brighton, Sussex, Surrey and London over an eighteen-month period, accumulating a £700,000 haul.

Despite wearing a mask, gloves and two pairs of trousers, Saunders could not disguise his distinctive, bow-legged walk, attributed to a physical deformity known as 'genu varum'. Saunders' distinctive walk was captured on many CCTV cameras during the robberies, and investigators enlisted the help of podiatrist and gait analyst Dr Haydn Kelly. He was asked to view the CCTV footage from the robberies and also separate footage of the suspect, Saunders, taken from police surveillance. Dr Kelly was able to confirm that the footage was of the same individual with the genu varum condition; only 5 per cent of the population displays this same distinctive 'John Wayne' gait.

Saunders' conviction is the first case of its kind in the UK to use gait analysis as a forensic discipline, but the evidential value of footwear marks is by no means a new practice. The first recorded case involving footwear evidence in a criminal case can be traced back to Scotland in the autumn of 1786. After returning home from harvesting their fields, a couple returned to their cottage in the parish of Kirkcudbright, Dumfries, and discovered their daughter had been murdered – her throat had been cut.

Surgeons subsequently discovered that the young girl was pregnant, and were also able to surmise that her assailant was left-handed due to the slashing nature of the fatal infliction. At the scene a bloodied handprint was discovered, and also a footwear mark left in the soft ground that surrounded the cottage. The gait and pacing of the footwear marks suggested they were left by someone fleeing the scene, and a crude attempt was made to recover a plaster cast of the footwear impression for future comparison to any suspect's shoes.

It was concluded that the footwear marks had been made with a boot that had recently been repaired, due to the new soles and nail marks visible on the cast. Following the young girl's funeral, investigators called for all the men who had attended to show their boots so they could be compared and measured. William Richardson's boot had features on the sole that were similar to the crime scene mark, and a cobbler later confirmed that he had recently carried out repairs to those same boots.

Following his arrest, Richardson was also discovered to have sustained scratches to his face, and he was found to be left-handed. Further evidence came to light that proved Richardson's guilt: prior to his execution, he confessed to the murder and revealed the whereabouts of the murder weapon. He stated that the motivation for the murder had been his shame in paying attention to and associating with a woman of 'weak intellect'. He clearly wasn't very smart himself!

FOOTWEAR AND CHARACTER LIFESTYLE

If it is an imperative part of your plot for a character to leave some form of footwear evidence, it is worth ensuring that the footwear involved is in keeping with their personality. For example, if your protagonist is a high-flying, well-heeled business person it is unlikely they will be wearing a cheap pair of Reebok classics, while the petty crook living hand to mouth is not going to be wearing a pair of Louboutins.

Imported shoes may not be stored on any form or UK footwear database, although this in itself may make that particular shoe and pattern unique if there are not many examples of that particular brand being worn over here. Brand new footwear is going to have weaker evidential footwear than worn shoes, but not everybody can afford to buy new shoes – these are things you need to consider to ensure your plot line remains plausible and is in keeping with your character's lifestyle.

DEPOSITING FOOTWEAR MARKS

When footwear marks are deposited in a crime scene they may be two- or three-dimensional, depending on the type of surface on which they are found. Three-dimensional marks are referred to as impressed marks, such as those found in soil, sand, wet concrete or even snow. Two-dimensional marks are known as surface transfer marks, and may be visible if they have been left in a contaminant such as blood, paint or dust. Latent surface transfer marks may only become apparent following the application of fingerprint or chemical treatments, various light sources or luminol.

A footwear mark may be discovered on a newspaper or magazine, in which case the item can be physically recovered for comparison to the suspect mark. However, the evidential value of such a movable item will always be questionable, as it could have been an opportunity for your characters to deliberately leave false evidence in a crime scene.

Crime scene investigators and forensic laboratory staff have a variety of methods available to them to record and recover footwear evidence from scenes, but before we look at these, it is useful to consider the types of surface on which you, as a writer, might wish to deposit your antagonist's mark in order to suit your storyline.

The footwear marks left, like those in real life, may be full, partial or fragmented impressions. The list of surfaces below offers some suggestions, but is in no way exhaustive – these are typically the kinds of surface from which I have recovered footwear marks at real crime scenes:

- window ledges (interior and exterior)
- kitchen work surfaces
- vehicles (floor mats, bonnets, roof, windscreens)
- shop counters (including screens in petrol stations and banks)
- floors of various textures
- chairs
- bedding
- clothing
- paperwork
- drainpipes
- wheelie-bin lids
- doors and windows
- bodies

As already mentioned, the discovery of footwear marks in a crime scene can help investigators estimate the minimum number of people involved and also their movements in the crime scene. Finding footwear marks on a body is no different, whether those impressions are recorded on a victim who is lying in intensive care or being examined in the mortuary.

During a violent assault it is not uncommon for offenders to resort to kicking and stamping on their victims. I have known many cases where the victim has been kicked about the torso or had their head repeatedly stamped on. But the body, like any other surface, is capable of retaining clear, identifiable footwear impressions from the offender's shoe/s, thereby providing information regarding the number of offenders involved and the ferocity of the attack.

Many offenders claim to have stood on the victim's face accidentally during the attack, whereas they were actually repeatedly stamped on. This is often corroborated by witness statements, which often describe how the victim's head was 'kicked like a football'.

RECOVERING FOOTWEAR MARKS

Footwear marks are recorded and recovered in a variety of ways, depending on whether they are two-dimensional or three-dimensional.

Two-Dimensional Footwear Marks

The methods available for searching for, enhancing and recovering two-dimensional footwear marks are very similar to the techniques employed when recovering latent fingerprints. A thorough visual examination using a good light source is a valuable starting point, and then the crime scene investigator will adopt the most effective method of recovery, depending on the location and texture of the mark in question.

The mark may be photographically recorded with and without a scale at a 90-degree angle, to provide the best 1:1 comparison for the footwear specialist to use. If the mark requires enhancing, then contrasting fingerprint powders can be used, depending on the type of surface the mark has been deposited on. Alternatively the forensic laboratory may attend to assist with alternative light sources and the application of chemical treatments.

The footwear mark can be 'lifted' in a way similar to a fingerprint lift, by using a piece of fablon: this is clear, thin plastic, slightly larger and narrower than a sheet of A4 paper, with a tape-like coating, which can lift the mark and is then covered with the clear plastic sheet – fablon lifts are used to recover any footwear

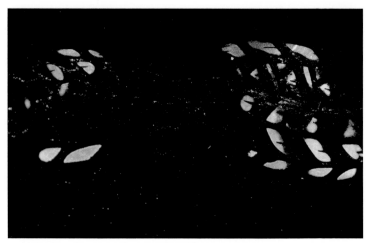

Gel lift of a white granular powdered footwear mark.

marks enhanced using flake powder such as aluminium. If the mark is enhanced using granular powder, it can be recovered using a 'gel' lift. This is of similar size and shape to a fablon lift, but has a denser coating of black gel.

ESLA

If a two-dimensional mark has been left on a dusty surface, the crime scene investigator will recover it using a piece of equipment

Electrostatic lifting apparatus.

known as 'electrostatic lifting apparatus' (ESLA). This device produces voltage that can be applied to a piece of conductive foil. The film is placed over the dusty footwear mark, and the ESLA is positioned partly on a metal plate and partly on the foil. When the ESLA is turned on and the volts activated, the electric charge 'lifts' the dusty footwear mark, causing the mark to cling to the foil.

Three-Dimensional Footwear Marks

A three-dimensional mark left in soil or similar is recovered by casting, using a plaster-cast substance such as Kaffa D. The relevant footwear mark is exhibited and photographed, and then the casting solution is mixed in a bag with the required amount of water. Once mixed, it is poured into the impressed mark, and when it starts to harden, the crime scene investigator will score the cast with their exhibit reference number.

Once completely hardened, usually between thirty and sixty minutes depending on the weather conditions and the type of brand used, the cast will be removed from the soil and packaged in a sturdy box to prevent any damage. Undoubtedly soil will also be recovered with the footwear cast, and this is retained as part of the evidence, as traces of the same soil may be recovered on the soles of the suspect's shoe.

TYRE MARKS

If tyres are considered as a car's 'shoes', then we can treat them in much the same way as we deal with the forensic recovery of footwear. Treadmate is a reference database set up with the same intention as SoleMate. It stores details of tyre patterns from the information provided by manufacturers, and may subsequently provide links that are invaluable to a murder investigation.

Tyre marks are recorded using the same techniques as those used for footwear recovery. They can be photographically recorded on a 1:1 basis for scientific comparison, or cast using Kaffa D. As with footwear casts, the use of Kaffa D also allows the collection of soil samples, which increases the evidential link of the suspect vehicle in the crime scene. Tyres will incur the same accidental damage as footwear, which is what makes each tyre unique and potentially identifiable by the scientist.

The link between tyre marks and crime scenes was particularly relevant in the Yorkshire Ripper case. Serial killer Peter Sutcliffe, also known as the Yorkshire Ripper, was eventually apprehended

Tyre marks also have evidential value.

by police in 1981, having murdered thirteen women over a five-year period. He was also convicted of attempting to murder a further seven women, who miraculously survived his vicious attacks. During the course of the investigation, one of the many forensic clues gathered at the various crime scenes included tyre marks. Irene Richardson was brutally murdered by Sutcliffe in February 1977 at Roundhay Park, Leeds. Her mutilated remains were discovered at the location, and so were fresh tyre marks.

Later that same year, on 14 December 1977, Sutcliffe attacked Marilyn Moore on some wasteland behind a mill near Buslingthorpe Lane in Leeds. He attacked her with a hammer, but fortunately her screams caused him to fear he might be disturbed, so he fled the scene. Marilyn Moore survived the attack and was able to provide police with one of the best photofits at that stage in the investigation.

Whilst examining the crime scene, investigators discovered fresh tyre marks in mud, and these were later found to match the tyre marks discovered at Roundhay Park during the murder investigation of Irene Richardson. They later proved to be a match to the tyres of Sutcliffe's vehicle, a red Ford Corsair.

Sutcliffe is currently serving a whole life sentence in HM Prison Frankland in Durham.

THE BENEFITS OF FOOTWEAR

Cinderella's glass slipper should now seem more relevant to the story than ever before, given the potential evidential value of footwear in an investigation, whether it is the size, pattern or accidental characteristics of a shoe, or whether a distinctive brand can be linked to an individual through CCTV footage or witness statements. Shoes can be a source of DNA, or they may contain other valuable trace evidence, such as glass, fibres, soil or hair. Regardless of whether it amounts to conclusive evidence or a useful piece of intelligence, every piece of the investigative jigsaw is one step closer to closure in the fight against crime.

CHAPTER 7

Trace Evidence

In Chapter 3 we were introduced to Edmund Locard's theory of exchange, which states that 'every contact leaves a trace'. This chapter is an extension of that premise, as we delve further into the types of evidence from seemingly innocuous sources, which can potentially be woven into our plot lines. However, a word of caution – trace evidence is *not* routinely collected at every investigation.

It would be incorrect to portray a volume crime scene that is attended by a CSI who then proceeds to recover glass, paint, fibres and soil. This would only be done if there were a suspect in custody with tools and clothing that could be compared to the crime scene samples; otherwise it is a wasted, time-consuming exercise. In a murder investigation, however, trace evidence is recovered, and as the majority of crime writing involves a dead body, I would like to familiarize you with the types of sample you could be including in your writing.

At all times it is worth remembering that forensic evidence can be used to eliminate suspects, not just to convict them, so trace evidence, like any other evidence type, can be used at your writer's discretion to impact on your storyline. Just ensure that the evidence is used in a plausible and realistic manner, avoiding far-fetched scenarios and too much embellishment.

But for now, I have another modern-day adaptation of a fairytale for you to consider, which introduces the types of trace evidence we will be looking at in this chapter: Goldilocks and the Three Bears.

A MODERN-DAY FAIRYTALE

Not long after the three bears headed off for their pre-breakfast ramble, Goldilocks arrived at the cottage in her Volkswagen Beetle, parked up and made her way to the rear of the property. She knew the bears' greenhouse was overflowing with home-grown fruit and vegetables, and she wanted her share. She picked up a stone from the path and smashed the greenhouse window so she could climb in and fill her carrier bag with produce.

Next she made her way to the kitchen window, and taking out her screwdriver, proceeded to jemmy it open. Once inside she ate some porridge, sat on a few chairs, breaking one in the process, before having a quick power nap in one of the beds. She was rudely awoken by the sound of the bears arriving back home, and quickly escaped out of the bedroom window. Catching sight of the angry bears, she was in such a hurry to get away that she scraped her car against a nearby tree – but thankfully for her, still managed to get away.

She was later apprehended and arrested; her clothing and vehicle were seized, and her house was searched for evidence. Back at the bears' house the attending crime scene investigator was particularly interested in collecting samples of trace evidence from four areas: the glass from the broken window, soil samples from the greenhouse, tool marks from the jemmied kitchen window, and paint samples left on the tree from the speeding getaway vehicle. The trace evidence was mounting, and it looked as if Goldilocks would soon be eating a lot more porridge!

GLASS AS TRACE EVIDENCE

Broken glass gets everywhere! (I should know, from the number of times I've cut myself at scenes.) On a positive note, I've attended quite a few burglaries and robberies where offenders have cut themselves, and unwittingly bled through their gloves. Scientists also know just where broken glass can get and have conducted tests to discover how glass travels after it has been smashed, an occurrence known as backward fragmentation.

If your character smashes a window, most of the glass will travel in the direction it was broken; however, a percentage of it will travel backwards, known as backward fragmentation, up to a distance of three metres. This means there is more than enough opportunity for the person to be showered in up to a thousand glass fragments measuring as little as half a millimetre, which will become lodged in their hair, footwear and clothing.

Unfortunately the fragments can be shed quite quickly – the majority will be lost within the first hour. Bear in mind, however, that if your character leaves the scene in a vehicle shortly after smashing the window, then traces of the glass may be deposited on the seats, seatbelts, armrests and footwells. Likewise, if they enter another property then the trace evidence will be shed there, and it will be up to the crime scene investigator to find it.

The persistence of the glass fragments on clothing depends on what your character is wearing. Woollen or fleece-type clothing will retain glass twice as long as a smoother material such as denim or a waterproof jacket. Also traces may be found in cuffs and pockets some time later, as these areas afford any fragments a greater level of protection.

The location of glass fragments on the offender can affect the strength of the evidential value. For example, if the suspect has punched a window, then glass found on their gloves, hat or hair combings can indicate that they were present when the window was being smashed, and has stronger evidential value than glass found on the soles of their shoes. Also, the greater the amount of fragments discovered on a suspect or their clothing, the greater is the likelihood that they were present at the crime scene.

Crime scene investigators will obtain a control glass sample from the scene, which scientists can then compare to the fragments taken from the suspect. Scientists conduct a number of tests in order to ascertain if the suspect sample can be traced back to the crime scene. These tests include measuring the refractive index and the composition of the glass.

Assessing the Refractive Index Measurement of Glass

Refraction refers to the way a ray of light changes direction when it enters a medium such as water, or indeed glass, at an angle. A rainbow is caused by the refraction (as well as the reflection) of light as it is dispersed through water droplets. Another way to observe the effects of refraction is to place a straw into a glass of water, and you will see how the straw appears to bend.

Observing refraction – see how the straw appears to bend?

One of the defining features of glass is its refractive index. Scientists will take the glass sample and melt it in silicon oil. The refractive index of the warming oil is already known and is used as the measurement guide, so when the piece of glass appears to disappear in the oil, this gives the scientist its refractive index measurement (GRIM). If the control sample reaches the same refractive measurement, it can be indicative that the two samples are from the same source.

The Composition of Glass
Glass is a fusion of sand, limestone and soda. Depending on the function of the glass, other chemicals can be added, such as iron oxide, which acts as a lubricant and causes glass to have a bluish/green tint. Aluminium oxide is added to strengthen glass so it is more scratchproof and less likely to shatter.

Additives are sometimes purposely added to colour glass to make it more ornamental or functional, for example wine-bottle green. When scientists compare glass from the scene and the control sample, these additives will enable them to ascertain if they are from the same source.

The density of the glass is another comparable feature, which scientists can use as a measuring tool by weighing the mass and volume of the samples. The density of the glass alters depending on where it is from – for example, toughened glass from a car windshield will be denser than the glass used to make a wine glass. The appearance of these two types is noticeably different – glass from a car windscreen will 'pebble' into chunkier, denser pieces, whereas a wine glass will shatter into thinner, sharper shards.

Whether the samples of glass are flat or rounded can also indicate their source, whether they have come from the flat surface area of a window or the rounded/curved surface of a bottle or the casing of a vehicle light. The scientist's ability to conclusively determine that *all* these factors match the two samples carries strong evidential value in the investigation.

Glass as Evidence
If you intend to use glass as an essential piece of evidence, it is worth considering the origin of the source. Has your victim been attacked with a glass bottle or vase, or have they been thrown through a glass window? The glass could come from an ornament, a picture frame or even a mirror. It will be more easily identifiable and unique if it originates from a stained glass window, or is patterned or wired.

Coloured and patterned glass has stronger evidential value.

It may be possible for the suspect sample and the control sample to be matched because they can be paired to make a physical fit. If there has been a road traffic accident, the discarded remains of a vehicle's headlight may later be matched to the offending vehicle by physical fit. Likewise, the neck of a broken beer bottle may be paired to the base.

Also, remember to consider other evidence types that may be recovered from the glass. A drinking glass or bottle may provide traces of saliva. As discussed earlier, broken glass may also contain traces of blood. Fingerprints may be evident, though remember to consider the size of the surface area – if it is too small it will not allow enough identifiable ridge detail to be deposited. Also, if the glass is fractured, then this will distort the ridge detail, making it difficult to analyse. Traces of footwear may be found on more complete pieces of glass that have been trodden on, such as picture frames.

SOIL AS TRACE EVIDENCE

The case involving murderer Ian Huntley demonstrates how soil analysis contributed to his conviction.

On 4 August 2002, ten-year-old Holly Wells and Jessie Chapman from Soham in Cambridgeshire went missing. Tragically, their bodies were found abandoned in a drainage ditch near RAF

Lakenheath, Suffolk. They had been murdered by Ian Huntley in his home, which he shared with their former teaching assistant, Maxine Carr. Huntley killed the two girls and later disposed of their bodies.

Following the discovery of their bodies on 17 August, a forensic ecologist was one of the many experts tasked with examining the crime scene. The ecologist noticed that nettles surrounding the ditch had developed side shoots, which suggested they had been trodden on, encouraging them to reshoot. This information enabled investigators to conclude that the damaged nettles represented the path Huntley had taken to dispose of the bodies in the ditch.

Furthermore, the ecologist could surmise that the side shoots had taken thirteen days to reach that stage of growth, which coincided with the timeline of the murders. As if this evidence wasn't compelling enough, the ecologist also examined soil samples taken from the scene with soil samples taken from Huntley's footwear and his Ford Fiesta, and the comparison allowed them to conclude that Huntley had been to the indicated deposition site, some twelve miles away from his home.

Traces of soil can often be found on clothing, shoes and tyres, but items such as spades and pickaxes should also be considered. As with glass, it is the distribution of the soil traces that can piece together a sequence of events, and not just the chemical composition of the samples. For example, do soil smears on the knee and elbow areas of a suspect's clothing, as well as contact traces on the

Soil and vegetation can be valuable sources of trace evidence.

top of the shoes, indicate that they were positioned on hands and knees at some point? Traces of soil on the rim of a spade can prove that that spade was used at the location of a burial site. And it is not just soil that can be considered a valuable source of trace evidence: pollen, vegetation and wood can be too.

Soil consists of a mixture of minerals, water, gases and organic matters, and its location will also dictate the quantity of clay, silt or sand in its composition. It can vary greatly in colour and texture, and there may be many factors involved in its distribution and location. For example, planting bedding plants into a flowerbed introduces a different type of soil, which would not necessarily be found in the original flowerbed. Soil from the original source may be found to be more acidic than soil from the introduced plants. It is the complexity of the composition of soil that can actually make it a unique piece of trace evidence.

TOOL MARKS AS TRACE EVIDENCE

Tool marks are usually taken into consideration at a volume crime scene when there has been a burglary. If there is a sequence of linked burglaries and a suspect has been arrested, crime scene investigators will attend and record the damage and the marks made by the tool at the scene, for comparison to any instruments found on the suspect. If a suspect has forced their way into a murder victim's house, then there is all the more reason to locate, record and recover any instrument marks at the point of entry.

When a tool is pressed against a surface, as long as the instrument doesn't make a dragging motion, like a saw, then it is highly likely that it will leave a three-dimensional mark in the surface. For example, when a screwdriver is used to jemmy open a window, the edge of the screwdriver will cause an indentation in the frame, which can then be compared to the offending tool.

A saw, and similar tools such as a plane, will not produce an indentation in use as the repetitive motion will prevent any such indentation from forming on the surface. The saw itself, however, may pick up traces of wood or paint, which can still be used for comparison purposes, proving that it was probably used at the crime scene.

Tool marks found at a crime scene can be recorded photographically on a 1:1 basis, with and without a scale, to allow scientists to make a direct comparison with the instrument in question. The crime scene investigator also has the option to 'cast' the tool mark using putty or casting equipment such as Provil. Casting the mark

A screwdriver with striation marks and traces of grease.

means that the unique striations of the tool – such as, for example, a flat-headed screwdriver – can be seen and compared directly to the instrument by the scientist, by physical fit and microscopic examination.

The casting process conducted by the crime scene investigator involves applying the casting medium into the aperture left by the instrument – say, a screwdriver – and leaving it to set. Just as with footwear casts, the setting of the medium depends on the particular brand being used, and the weather conditions. Once it has set, it can be peeled away from the instrument mark and submitted to the laboratory with the suspect screwdriver.

Scientists can also compare the scarring caused by instrument marks by making a test mark using the tool and comparing it to the scene sample. Further comparison is then made under the microscope. It may be that scientists make a test mark into a soft metal such as lead, which is sufficiently malleable to retain the striation marks made by the instrument.

Certain cutting instruments can be compared directly to other items to prove that they have been used to gain access to a scene. An example would be comparing the scarring caused by a pair of bolt cutters to a thick metal chain or padlock, which had secured access to a property. Pliers may also be compared to leads and cables that have been cut, and it may be that a piece of plastic from a cable has been retained in the pliers.

When comparing tool marks, the same level of evidential value applies as it did when comparing footwear marks. The older the tool, inevitably the more worn it will be, and the more marks it will have incurred through accidental damage, which the scientist can compare with the scene marks. The tool may also have picked up traces of paint from, say, a window frame, which introduces another element of trace evidence to compare, and doubles its evidential value for conclusively linking it to a scene.

THE FORENSIC METALLURGIST

Another specialist role to be aware of is that of the forensic metallurgist, and also their potential contribution to a criminal investigation. They may also become involved as part of an investigation by the Health & Safety Executive following a fatal or life-changing works accident. Metallurgy is the scientific study of metal and the method of its production and properties. Forensic metallurgy concerns itself with investigating why things have failed and subsequently resulted in a loss of life, and whether such a failure was due to natural metal fatigue, human error or criminality.

PAINT AS TRACE EVIDENCE

The case involving murderer Gary Ridgway demonstrates how paint analysis was a deciding factor in his conviction.

Dubbed the Green River Killer after the name of the location where his victims were found, Gary Ridgway is an American serial killer from Utah. He was convicted of forty-nine murders, but is believed to have committed more than twice that number. He was most prolific in crime in the 1980s and 1990s, mainly targeting prostitutes. It was believed that in addition to raping, beating and murdering his victims (usually by strangulation), Ridgway returned to the bodies and continued to have intercourse with them.

Ridgway was arrested in 2001 after DNA samples originally seized from his victims in 1987 were subjected to DNA testing, thanks to the advances made in profiling. In addition to the damning DNA evidence, investigators were also able to match small traces of spray paint from some of the victims' clothing. This paint was later conclusively matched to the specialist spray paint used at the Renton Washington Kenworth Truck Factory, where Ridgway worked as a painter.

Ridgway eventually confessed to his crimes, which included rape, murder and necrophilia, and only avoided the death penalty because he agreed to cooperate fully with the investigation and to locate the bodies of his victims. Aged fifty-four, he was sentenced to 480 years' imprisonment on 18 December 2003.

Whether it is wet or dry, paint has the potential to be transferred from crime scenes in a multitude of scenarios. It can be chipped from window frames during burglaries, transferred from vehicles during road traffic collisions, or just physically transferred from an individual via their clothing, as detailed in the case of the Green River Killer. Paint is everywhere, which makes it a good source of trace evidence to include in any storyline.

Chipped, flaking paint will persist in a similar manner to glass fragments, whereas wet paint or paint transferred following a vehicle collision will obviously persist longer. The circumstances surrounding the transfer may mean that only the top coat is present at the scene; in other cases, multiple layers are present.

There may also be an opportunity to make a physical fit comparison, depending on the situation. Scientists can compare the chemical composition of paint, particularly the pigmentation, and use it to link a suspect to a scene. Various paint suppliers maintain reference databases, which can assist scientists in comparing and identifying various sources of paint. This facility was used in the case described below, when the link between paint samples led to the conviction of Malcolm Fairley.

Malcolm Fairley, also known as 'The Fox', was a serial rapist who was active in Buckinghamshire and Bedfordshire in 1984. He committed the majority of his attacks after breaking into people's properties whilst brandishing a shotgun. He took pains to disguise himself by wearing makeshift masks cut from pieces of clothing. Following one rape, he cut a section of quilt from the scene and buried it, in an attempt to avoid leaving his semen at the scene.

After fleeing the scene of one of his victim's houses in Brampton-en-le-Morthen, South Yorkshire, he accidentally collided into a tree whilst driving away. Investigators were able to recover paint samples at the scene, which they subsequently had analysed. The paint was matched to that used by British Leyland, in particular the brand Harvest Yellow, which was used on the Austin Allegro model manufactured between 1973 and 1975.

Once the make and model of the car were known, it was down to detectives to investigate the several hundred owners of such a vehicle. Their investigations eventually led them to Fairley's house, where they discovered the vehicle bearing damaged paintwork consistent with the damage from the scene. In addition to this, they found items of clothing in the boot that had pieces missing, from

The more layers of paint, the stronger the evidential value.

which Fairley had created his homemade masks. He was arrested on 11 September 1984 at his London home.

FIBRES AS TRACE EVIDENCE

Fibres are a common type of trace evidence recovered from crime scenes, as they are easily shed and transferred depending on the circumstances of the crime and the level of prolonged contact. Fibres fall into two categories, natural and artificial:

Natural: silk, cotton, wool, cashmere, flax, mohair
Artificial: rayon, spandex, acrylic, polyester, nylon, viscose

I have listed these examples to encourage you to think which types of fibre your characters might realistically shed at a crime scene. Staying true to your character's persona and depending on their lifestyle, age, affluence and fashion sense, are they likely to wear something distinctive and prone to shedding, such as an angora sweater, or a nylon sports jacket? Is the fibre transfer going to be from clothing, or from a rug or carpet, car seats, teddy bears, dolls, bedding, or curtains that have been used to wrap a body in?

As with all the other trace evidence we have detailed so far, it is the amount, distribution and apparent uniqueness of the fibre evidence that will determine its value. Whatever the circumstances your character finds themselves in, you must ensure that the traces, persistence, transfer and detection of the evidence remain plausible.

Persistence and Recovery of Fibres

The persistence of fibres has many variables: it depends on the two types of surface involved in the transfer, the level and repeated amount of contact, and the time interval between contact occurring at the crime scene and recovery. Scientific tests have shown that an average of 3 per cent of fibres will persist on a piece of clothing for thirty hours after contact.

However, this varies depending on the material involved, also whether the clothing has been continuously worn, if other clothing has been placed on top of it, if the item has been washed, and the activity of the wearer – whether the clothing has had prolonged contact with other surfaces, or been exposed to inclement weather. Obviously, the persistence of fibres on other surfaces, such as seats, bedding or carpet, will differ – again depending on a number of variables.

The amount of fibre present tends to dictate the method of recovery. Clumps of fibre can be recovered using tweezers and packaged appropriately. If the fibres are in a more fragile area and risk being lost, or if the crime scene investigator or scientist is conducting a speculative search, then a tape lift will be used. This involves taking a section of low-tack adhesive tape and pressing it against the surface containing the fibres, thereby recovering them. The tape

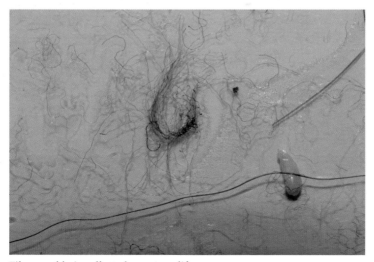

Fibres and hair collected on a tape lift.

lift will then be placed on a clear piece of plastic sheeting such as Cobex, and exhibited and secured in an evidence bag. Scientists will microscopically examine the fibres in order to ascertain a match.

HAIR

As well as being a source of DNA, hair can also be regarded as trace evidence because of its propensity to shed; it is quite common to find traces of hair on clothing, bedding, vehicles and so on. Hair can be recovered in the same way as fibres, depending on the amount and the location. Whether that hair is from a human or animal can also be of strong evidential value in your investigation. In the case described below the suspect was convicted following the recovery of some of the murderer's head hairs on the victim's body.

Leanne Tiernan, a sixteen-year-old schoolgirl from Leeds, went missing on 26 November 2000. Her remains were discovered some ten miles away in Lindley Woods near Otley by a dog walker. It was evident that Leanne had been strangled, and police believed her body had been kept in cold storage for some time. Her body had been wrapped in bedding and green bin liners secured with twine, and her head covered with a plastic bag secured using a dog collar. She had a scarf and cable tie around her neck, and her wrists were bound with the same type of cable ties.

The trace evidence recovered from Leanne's body, as well as DNA evidence, was damning in identifying the murderer, John Taylor. Scientists from Texas were called upon to produce a partial dog profile from the hairs, but the evidence could not be used as Taylor's dog had died.

Taylor was matched to the scene after enquiries linked him to the sale of the dog collar found on Leanne's body. One of his head hairs was also found on her scarf, and his profile was extracted using mitochondrial DNA testing. The twine and cable ties were traced back to their original source of manufacture, and conclusively matched to being the same as those discovered in Taylor's house. Red nylon fibres from a carpet, which he had since attempted to dispose of, were also discovered on Leanne, as well as pieces of plastic that matched the green bin bags she had been wrapped in.

Traces of pollen found in Leanne's nasal passages could also be matched to traces found in Taylor's garden at the time the schoolgirl had gone missing. Furthermore, police discovered three chest freezers at Taylor's home, which is believed to be where he had stored Leanne's body for several months prior to dumping her in Lindley Woods. In July 2002, Taylor pleaded guilty to abduction and murder, and was awarded life with a minimum of thirty years; it is to be hoped that he will never be released.

ANTI-INTRUDER DEVICES

Anti-intruder devices are designed to discourage would-be thieves by coating them in a particular substance once they attempt to enter a property. This substance can be as basic as anti-vandal paint, or it may be a more sophisticated product such as SmartWater or Smoke-Cloak.

SmartWater is the trade name of a traceable, liquid deterrent invented in the 1990s by a retired police officer and his chemist brother. In short, the product contains a chemical signature, which can be used with a specially adapted pen to mark property (usually with a postcode) so it can be traced back to its original owner in the event of the property being stolen. The chemical solution fluoresces under ultra-violet light, but is effectively invisible to the naked eye when not fluoresced. It can also be applied through a sprinkler system, which coats the intruder in the invisible liquid if they break into the property. SmartWater solution is very resilient and difficult to remove, and can persist for up to five years. Custody suites in police stations have purpose-built ultra-violet screening, so prisoners can be screened on their arrival. Similar brands include SelectaDNA and Microdot.

SmokeCloak works by filling a property with an impenetrable cloud of fog when a break-in occurs. By significantly reducing visibility, the cloak disorientates the burglar and makes it impossible for them to search for property, let alone find their way round, so they have no option but to flee. SmokeCloak DNA combines the effectiveness of SmokeCloak with the added bonus of applying a traceable liquid to the intruders for future detection, providing an overwhelming source of trace evidence.

THE BENEFITS OF TRACE EVIDENCE

Using trace evidence in your storyline is always worth considering, as the choices available are many and it can be easily introduced. Don't feel restricted regarding the type of trace evidence, but consider all the sources available: these include wallpaper, plaster, oil, gunshot residue, accelerants, possibly even make-up. I can't reiterate enough, that as long as your trace evidence is deposited and recovered in a realistic, plausible manner, then the options are endless.

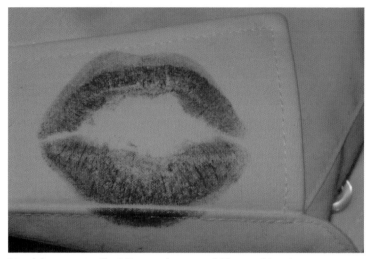

Lipstick on your collar? Even make-up could be considered trace evidence.

When it comes to your crime scene investigator or detective recovering the trace evidence, always remember the rules regarding cross contamination. If your character is the detective or CSI who has attended the crime scene, the same person cannot recover clothing or hair combings from the suspect in custody, nor can they take any part in the examination of the suspect's house or vehicle.

The evidential value of trace evidence will depend upon how rare it is, and whether there is something distinctive about it to make it distinguishable to a similar medium of its type, such as wood. You will also need to consider the possibility of accidental contamination, and whether the trace evidence can conclusively place an offender in a scene, or if it has been transferred by genuine means.

CHAPTER 8

Fire Scenes

In the early hours of Sunday, 2 September 1666 a fire started in the King's Bakery on Pudding Lane in London. Due to the extremely hot and dry summer that year there was a drought in the city, and the parched wooden buildings acted as little more than kindling: the fire quickly grew. Historically it became known as the Great Fire of London. Due to the close proximity of all the other buildings and houses, plus the combination of the strong east wind fanning the flames, the rabbit warren streets of London were soon ablaze and the majority of the city was razed to the ground. Despite the fire being brought under control several days after it started, it is probable that the city continued to smoulder for several weeks afterwards.

Although the cause of the fire was in fact accidental, the people of London sincerely believed that this fire, which had such devastating consequences right across their great city, was a deliberate act of terrorism, believed to have been carried out by the French or the Dutch. Such conspiracy theories bring us to the purpose of this chapter, which looks at how fire scenes are investigated and whether or not they can be regarded as having been started accidentally or deliberately – in other words, if they are arson. This is important so that such fire scenes can be accurately portrayed and described in your writing.

Fire scenes are without doubt one of the most problematic crime scenes to investigate. There are health and safety implications surrounding the structure of the building and whether it is safe to enter, and further complications may arise if the building is suspected to contain asbestos. Smoke and water can, in some cases, cause more damage than the actual fire.

The blackened charring of the room, combined with the lack of electricity, means the room is dark, so tripping is a serious hazard as the majority of the plaster from the ceiling and the walls will now be covering the floor. Water will still be dripping all around, and there will be puddles on the floor. Identifying the melted remains to establish what type of furnishing or item they once were is a slow and painstaking process. But despite the extensive amount of damage and destruction encountered at the majority of fire scenes, there are always clues to be found – and where there are clues, there are characters just waiting to happen.

FIRE SCIENCE

In order to appreciate how fires are investigated, we need first to consider the science behind how a fire is started. In order to get a fire started we need fuel, oxygen and heat – this was originally visualized in the form of a pyramid or a fire triangle. However, for anyone who has ever attempted to light a fire, you will know that in order to keep it burning, you need to adhere to the rules of combustion. This rule adds a fourth element, the chemical chain reaction, which is necessary to maintain the fire.

The fire tetrahedron pictured (also known as the fire diamond) visually demonstrates the four components needed to allow combustion. If any one of the four components is removed or reduced, then the fire can be controlled.

Fuel

Sources of fuel can be solid, liquid or gas. Liquid and solid fuels are sustained by a process known as pyrolysis, which is a thermo-chemical form of degradation: when a liquid or solid material is exposed to extreme heat, flammable vapours are released, which fuels the fire. Gas burns when mixed with the appropriate amount of air. In basic terms, if you have a substance that can be ignited and then continues to burn, it is considered fuel.

This allows you to introduce a multitude of materials that could be used to start or feed a fire. However, you should research the era you are writing in, as certain clothing and furnishings that are manufactured today must adhere to strict guidelines to ensure that they are fire retardant. These regulations would not have existed prior to the 1980s, however, and everyday objects, such as a horse-hair mattress or sofa, were renowned for being ignited through a carelessly discarded cigarette. In the right conditions they would have continued to smoulder before eventually catching alight and spreading to the rest of the room – and once the fire caught other flammable surfaces, such as the carpet and curtains, it would quickly develop.

Oxygen

Oxygen also acts as fuel to a fire if the mixture of air is at the correct ratio to cause effective combustion. Too much air can cause

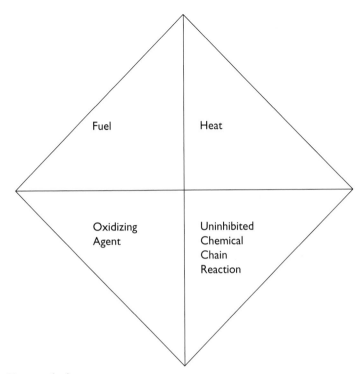

Fire tetrahedron.

the fire to be extinguished, while too little means the fire will be starved and will not be able to develop. Whilst oxygen is considered to be the usual component involved in combustion, it is useful to know that there are other oxidizing agents, such as hydrogen peroxide, and that certain chemicals also have an oxidizing effect, such as percholorates, used to propel fireworks.

Heat

During combustion, heat acts as an energy source. This activity causes an increase in ignition, vapour release, and growth of the fire. Heat is transferred through conduction, convection or radiation. The manner in which these three methods cause it to be transferred plays a fundamental part in assisting fire-scene investigators to interpret the source, cause and spread of the fire.

Conduction is the transfer of heat through other materials it is in contact with, typically a solid medium, such as metal. Convection is the transfer of heat through gases and fluids causing cooler particles to be heated through energy, causing them to become less dense as the heat increases. Radiation is the transmission of heat energy to a colder medium via electro-magnetic waves. Unlike conduction and convection, radiation does not require there to be direct contact between other particles to act as a medium for it to heat.

Chemical Chain Reaction

As already identified, three elements are necessary to start a fire, namely heat, fuel and oxygen. The fourth element, the chemical chain reaction, is the process of allowing the un-inhibition of the cycle to enable combustion to proceed.

This allows an exothermic reaction to occur – this is the chemical reaction, which must be self-sustaining and results in the release of light and heat. Simply put, the source of fuel is heated, resulting in ignition because of the presence of oxygen and with the addition of the energy from the heat transfer. This results in the production of heat and light, and the fire will continue to burn if all the required elements are suitably sustained.

You may wonder why fire science is relevant to you as an author. I can explain why, by describing where fires have accidentally thrived, or alternatively failed to catch on (much to the frustration of the arsonist). This occurs because of the lack of knowledge concerning the aforementioned fire tetrahedron, and may be relevant to you if you want to include a fire in your storyline, and are planning for the fire to fail or thrive.

After scenes involving shooting incidents, fire scenes are typically the next that are the most inaccurately portrayed on screen. I can appreciate that this is probably due to editors wishing to ensure an on-screen effect of maximum drama, and relies on the audience being so engrossed that they don't question the end result. As a writer, however, it is your responsibility to ensure that you couple veracity with drama – because if *you* don't, your competitors will.

Picture a typical action movie scene where guns are indiscriminately fired and cars and buildings are being blown up all over the place. The hero heads to where the bad guys are hiding out and hurls a petrol bomb through the window, which causes the building to become instantly consumed in flames. The bad guys die, the hero wins, and the fire continues to rage on, but with a suspicious lack of smoke: suspicious because as the saying goes, there's no smoke without fire – and this is true, except in movieland!

A petrol bomb is made by pouring a flammable substance into a bottle, adding a cloth or paper to act as a wick, which is then ignited and the bomb thrown, with the intention of setting fire to its target.

I have attended many scenes where this scenario has been committed with the intention of causing utter devastation. Fortunately, in the majority of cases, the wick will fail to maintain ignition, and the petrol bomb itself, if it has been ignited, will just burn itself out because the elements already discussed are not in a sustained state of equilibrium to be effective; this explains why the above movie scenario is not always portrayed accurately.

Probably one of the most shocking and horrific crimes so far this decade is the case of arson committed in May 2012 by Michael Philpott, his wife Mairead and their family friend, Paul Mosley. The fire took hold much more quickly than the arsonists expected, and tragically resulted in the death of six children, aged between five and thirteen. Prior to this awful event, Philpott was no stranger to the media, having become notorious for fathering up to seventeen children, whom he supported by claiming state benefits rather than working for a living. He appeared to adore the notoriety he received from the general public and the media, which included exposure on *The Jeremy Kyle Show* and a documentary looking at the 'benefits culture'. His arrogance in the face of such exposure was indicative of his personality: Philpott was a violent, domineering bully who historically controlled and assaulted his partners, while seeming to have little or no consideration or appreciation for the precious gift of parenthood.

The fire was deliberately staged with the intention of framing Philpott's ex-partner, with whom he and Mairead had shared the family home, prior to her leaving with her children in February 2012. The fire was started by Michael and Mairead Philpott and Paul Mosley to coincide with a custody hearing the morning of the fire, which they hoped would implicate Philpott's ex-partner and result in them maintaining full custody of his children.

Unfortunately for the six innocent children, Philpott's plan failed, with devastating results. The intention was to start the fire by pouring an accelerant through the letterbox. A ladder had already been strategically placed next to the children's bedroom window to allow Philpott to perform the role of rescuer, hero and devoted father. However, the accelerant took hold much more quickly than expected, and the house was engulfed so fast there was no hope for the children. Five of them perished in the fire, and the eldest lost his fight for life three days later in hospital.

The prison sentences awarded were issued on the conviction of manslaughter, as none of the arsonists allegedly anticipated causing the death of the children, so according to the law the charge of murder could not apply. The speed with which a fire can take hold

and spread clearly never occurred to them, and as a result, six innocent children lost their lives.

FIRE DEVELOPMENT

Now we know the theory behind fire science, we can look at the
four stages of fire development. Recognizing each stage allows you
to describe with accuracy how a fire can quickly increase; later we
will discuss fire characteristics, which will provide you with an
opportunity to describe accurately the visual features of a fire scene.

Incipient stage: Also known as ignition, this first stage begins
when all four components discussed in the fire tetrahedron have
resulted in a fire starting. This first stage is the easiest to control and
extinguish, and given the right circumstances, may possibly burn
out on its own accord before it has a chance to reach the second
stage.

Growth stage: This is the shortest but most sudden of the four
stages. The combination of oxygen and any nearby combustible material will fuel the fire. As it progresses, gases will rapidly
increase in temperature, resulting in a build-up of pressure in the
room.

Fully developed stage: When all the combustible materials have
been consumed the fire is at its peak and will be fully developed.
At this stage the heat will be immense, and because the room will
be engulfed in flames there will be little hope of escape or survival.

Decay stage: If the fire is left, then this final stage will be the long-
est, as the fire gradually finishes its consumption – think of a bonfire
that is left to burn. The heat in the final stage still remains intense,
and will do for some time, which is why firefighters remain so long
at a fire scene even after the flames have been extinguished. The fire
may continue to smoulder and there is a risk of pyrolysis occurring,
which may result in a secondary fire.

FIRE CHARACTERISTICS

Smouldering can be considered one of the characteristics of a fire.
Other fire characteristics exist and may occur during any of the four
stages, depending on the situation. One of the most dramatic stages
became the subject of a movie released in 1991 called *Backdraft*.

The colour
of flames can
differ.

A backdraft occurs when there is a sudden introduction of air to a fire that is in a confined space with no ventilation. The cycle is identified by yellow or brown smoke, and windows and doors may vibrate with the pressure. The most dramatic characteristic of a backdraft is the sudden pulling of air into the area of containment, which is a precursor to a dramatic explosion.

A flashover has a similarly dramatic effect and occurs during the growth stage. Pyrolysis results in simultaneous ignition of a combustible material in an enclosed space. This can be identified by rolling flames or 'tongues' of fire, and a rapid build-up of heat as the fire surges up towards the ceiling.

Temperature and chemical composition can influence the colour of a flame, depending on the materials involved. For example carbon burns red, yellow or orange, burning lithium will produce a pink flame, whereas copper will burn with a green tinge. Because of the varied mix of chemicals, rubber will tend to burn with flames heavily tinged in black. Iron will emit orange flames when burning, and aluminium or magnesium will produce whiter flames, a similar colour to sparks from a sparkler.

FIRE SCENE INVESTIGATION

Before we take a brief look at the methods involved in investigating a fire scene, we need to consider some of the typical causes of fire, which can then become part of the plot or storyline. Fires can be accidental, caused by an electric fault, faulty wiring, discarded cigarettes or candles, sparks from welding machinery, combustibles near a heat source, chip-pan fires, a blocked chimney, carelessly discarded coal from barbeques – the reasons are endless.

Any of these suggestions can also be used to set a fire deliberately. In some instances it may not actually be possible for fire investigators to determine if the fire is deliberate or not, but ruling out the likelihood of accidental causes would strongly suggest that the cause was deliberate.

A multi-agency approach is usually taken when investigating a fire, particularly if it has resulted in fatalities. In all cases, however, the fire will be jointly investigated by the fire brigade and police. The fire service will have ownership of the property until the fire is out and the building is deemed safe to enter, and then the police will take over the investigation of potential criminal activity.

Interviews and witness statements will be taken to ascertain who saw and heard what, and lines of enquiry will include establishing if there were any signs of disturbance prior to the fire, or if the occupant was in debt or any kind of trouble. Nearby CCTV footage will be considered, and in the majority of cases this will also include accessing the CCTV from the attending fire pumps, as some of these are fitted with recording devices. The images they capture, or indeed witness evidence from crew members, are invaluable to the investigation as they can record the intensity and direction of the fire, and if anyone was seen running away or acting suspiciously. It is not uncommon to find that in certain situations, members of the public will approach the fire brigade with information rather than approaching the police, for fear of reprisal from involved parties.

The fire scene will be examined by a fire investigator from the fire brigade and a crime scene investigator. In extreme cases, usually when there is a fatality or if it is a high value fire, a fire scientist may also attend the scene and will take various samples, which can be reconstructed and tested in laboratory conditions. As always, the role of the crime scene investigator is to photographically record the scene and each part of the excavation, and appropriately package and recover any exhibits. Nylon bags are used to package items taken from the fire as they can contain any vapours that might be present on the exhibit.

The scene examination starts outside the property in question to establish if there were any obvious signs of forced entry, and to ascertain if damage to the property was caused due to criminal activity or by the firefighters accessing the scene. The perimeter of the scene is searched for any suspicious items such as lighters, matches, accelerant containers or broken glass. An accelerant can be any form of flammable material that can cause the spread of a fire, such as petrol or newspaper. Also remember that whatever form of accelerant is used, it can always become a source of trace evidence for later comparison to a suspect or a secondary scene.

Glass is a good source of evidence at a fire scene because its direction, colour and location can indicate signs of a break-in, and the heat and direction of the fire. If glass is blackened from smoke and has a smooth, possibly wavy edge, this suggests it was intact when the fire took hold. Alternatively the glass may be covered in a web of cracking, which indicates sudden cooling – most likely from a hoseful of water.

The focus of the scene investigation is obviously to determine the cause, and this can be revealed at the seat of the fire, also known as the point of origin. Even if the building is only a blackened shell, there are usually enough indicators in the charred room to help identify the point of origin, as this will be the area in the room that has sustained the majority of the heat damage.

Any remaining plastics, such as smoke alarms, curtain racks or light-bulb holders, will have melted towards the direction of the heat. Likewise, heavy charring found on skirting boards, floorboards or furniture points towards the source. Experienced investigators are also trained in identifying the V pattern that can be found on vertical surfaces such as furniture, walls or doors, and which may point towards the source.

If a liquid accelerant has been used there may be traces of circular patterns known as pool burns. If several seats of fire can be identified this is a strong indication of deliberate ignition, and careful excavation of those areas usually provides extra clues. Excavation includes carefully removing the layers of debris from the point of origin and sieving through it: despite the intensity of the fire, items such as matches, cigarette ends or cigarette lighters are often still found intact, providing a source of fingerprint or DNA evidence.

Charring at a fire scene can provide clues as to its point of origin.

As the layers of debris are peeled away, investigators may suddenly notice a smell that could be from a potential liquid accelerant. I have attended many scenes where this is thought not to be present, but suddenly moving a piece of plasterboard or carpet releases the unmistakable whiff. When the seat of origin has been identified, the fire investigator may call on the assistance of a four-legged colleague, the arson dog.

These clever animals are trained to sniff out the smallest traces of accelerant, the presence of which they will indicate to their handler in exchange for a reward. They attend the scene wearing specialist made boots to prevent their paws getting cut on glass or other sharp debris that commonly occurs in a fire scene. Dogs are a valuable part of policing, as some are also trained to sniff out incendiary devices, cadavers, cash and drugs; they are also used in search and rescue efforts, when people have gone missing following an earthquake or on a mountain walk.

If the fire has started accidentally due to a discarded flame or cigarette, this can be quite evident; this is also the case with electrical faults. Examining what remains of electric sockets and items will piece together the cause of the fire. Likewise, if the fire resulted from a gas explosion, the examination of gas pipes and equipment will confirm this, and establish whether it was accidental or if it was set deliberately. If fire alarms and smoke detectors have remained intact and have not been tampered with, this suggests accidental ignition.

However, where smoke alarms have been damaged and entry obstructed, this suggests foul play. Investigators can quickly establish if items have been moved, stolen or disturbed because of smoke stencilling. Sometimes it is the absence of things in a property that helps paint a picture. If the fire has been started deliberately, perhaps for insurance purposes, it is highly likely that items of sentimental value such as photographs, jewellery and family pets will have been removed beforehand. Would your character be vicious enough to start a fire in the family home and leave the dog inside, just to free themselves from debt?

Examining fire scenes is such a huge and complex investigation, with the potential for so many variables, that it is really not possible to go into any further detail than I have here. However, I hope that being aware that investigators can determine whether a fire is accidental or deliberate, and that forensic and fingerprint evidence can still be recovered from the shell of a crime scene, gives you enough opportunity to help with your storyline. Whether your character chooses to set fire to clothing, vehicles, buildings or even bodies in an attempt to destroy evidence, this is not necessarily a foolproof plan.

CHAPTER 9

Drugs and Toxicology

One of my favourite childhood books was without doubt *Alice's Adventures in Wonderland*. It is one of those beautiful, intricate adventures, so suffused in the bizarre that it actually makes perfect sense – the unbelievable becomes believable. But the mind-bending hallucinations caused by Alice's indulgence, once she was tempted with 'eat me – drink me', is not such an innocent tale for those people whose lives have been marred by drug abuse and addiction.

In this chapter we will look at the different types of drug, their street names, what they look like and the typical methods of ingestion. By appreciating the effects of drugs and the power of addiction, we can begin to appreciate why seemingly ordinary people can be driven to extreme measures to feed their habit. The reality is that addiction is a very powerful motivator.

We will also consider the effects of toxicology, in case you intend your murder mystery to follow an Agatha Christie-type theme, and how your murderer can be traced back to the poisoned honeymoon meal he cooked for his wealthy new wife. We will look in more details at the toxicology samples that can be taken and the more famous cases involving poisoning, which can help fuel the writer's imagination.

There is, however, a caveat on the topic of drugs and toxicology, which I feel it is only responsible to point out. I will not go into detail as to how certain street drugs are taken, other than mentioning the type of equipment used when taking drugs. Likewise, although the issue of toxicology and fatalities may be discussed, I am obviously not going to reveal how to get hold of arsenic, how much is needed, or a 'serving suggestion' in order to kill someone.

I do not believe that certain fine details need to be researched or spelled out: rather, the power of suggestion and drama is all that is needed to make a storyline plausible. There are always certain aspects of DNA and fingerprint evidence available at drug scenes, but again, I will leave it to your discretion, based on the subjects covered in previous chapters, to hint at the necessary clues.

ADDICTION

Before we even start to look at identifying the types of drug and their classification, first we need to understand the psychology behind addiction, as this is the driver that keeps so many drug dealers – be they illegal or commercial – in business. Addiction is the physical or psychological dependence upon a habit-forming substance or activity. The repetition of a habit causes a synaptic pathway to build in the brain, which becomes rewarded by the release of dopamine – a neurotransmitter that controls reward and pleasure.

Compulsion fuels addiction, because with time, the consumption of a drug no longer results in the initial level of pleasure found when carving the synaptic pathway. Eventually, the addict is left with a void that they need to fill with more drugs in an attempt to fulfil the initial euphoric experience. Addiction also becomes a way of dealing with emotional stress, as the pleasure gained from the substance or activity in question numbs the brain from having to deal with reality and the rawness of an emotion – the addiction becomes a reaction to coping with stress.

Addiction eventually becomes so all-encompassing that even if the addict knows that indulging their habit may be severely detrimental to their health – even potentially fatal – these potential consequences are not as strong as the power of the compulsion. Given that these are the extremes that addicts are likely to face, it is little wonder the desperate acts they are willing to commit, and how low they are morally prepared to stoop, to ensure that their craving is met. People are willing to sell their bodies for sex, to steal or to deprive their own loved ones, or to commit heinous crimes, in order to acquire the money they need to fund their habit.

Whilst I passionately hate the damage that burglary and robbery have on innocent victims (both as a CSI and a victim of crime), I also have an element of sympathy for those whose addiction has led to a loss of self-respect and moral compass, and who are desperately reduced to committing such crimes. While in no way would I ever excuse the people who commit these crimes, and believe they should pay for the consequences, I recognize that rehabilitation is another precious commodity, which in modern-day society is hugely underfunded.

I struggled many years ago to give up smoking, and even now still find myself occasionally battling with the urge to reach for a cigarette, so I have the utmost respect for people who can give up Class A drugs, alcohol addiction and other vices. I would therefore urge you to consider that not all addicts are bad people. I don't think anyone ever sets out on purpose to become addicted to a substance or to an activity such as gambling. Perhaps my experiences over the years have allowed me to see both sides of the offence – the victim and the offender – and in order that you can write with conviction and empathy, I would suggest that you, too, consider this.

DRUG CLASSIFICATION

The Misuse of Drugs Act 1971 is the legislation responsible for classifying drugs into three categories. The classification of drugs depends on the amount of harm they are considered to cause to the user. The Misuse of Drugs Act also governs the production, supply, intent to supply and possession of drugs. Bear in mind that drugs can also include alcohol, tobacco and various prescription and non-prescription drugs, most typically painkillers such as codeine.

CLASS A DRUGS

This category lists all the drugs that are considered the most harmful. In addition to the ones mentioned below, any drug is considered Class A – even if it falls into a lower classification – if it is prepared in such a way that it is suitable for injection.

Possession of Class A drugs can result in up to seven years' imprisonment, an unlimited fine, or both. Production and supply can result in life imprisonment, an unlimited fine, or both.

Cocaine
Cocaine is a white powder that is typically snorted, although it can also be injected. Crack cocaine is a crystallized form of cocaine, which can be smoked. Street names include Charlie, snow, crack, freebase, rocks, wash and ching. Cocaine leaves the user feeling energized and confident, but its downside is the feeling of comedown afterwards, the risk of addiction, and displaying telltale 'gurning' or jaw clenching.

Heroin
Heroin is made from morphine, which is derived from the opium poppy. It comes in the form of a white or brown powder, and can be smoked, injected or snorted. Street names include smack, skag, gear and brown. Heroin provides the user with feelings of euphoria, followed by an intense feeling of relaxation.

Methadone
Methadone is a green liquid heroin substitute, which is medically

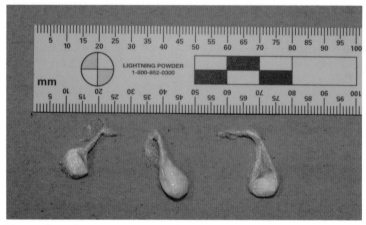

Wraps of cocaine.

prescribed to help wean heroin addicts off the drug in a controlled manner. It can also be illegally obtained and produced. It provides a similar sensation to heroin, but is less intense.

Ecstasy

Ecstasy gained its notoriety in the club scene during the eighties and nineties, as it provides users with an energy buzz that causes everything to feel more intense and euphoric; therefore not only could clubbers experience the ultimate party high, but they also had the energy to dance all night.

Known by the chemical name of MDMA, pure ecstasy comes in crystal powder form but is more commonly produced as pills that are stamped with various logos such as smiley faces and the Mitsubishi logo. Also known as E, ecstasy has a number of street names that typically relate to the tablet design, such as Rolex, Superman and dolphins.

Lysergic Acid Diethylamide (LSD)

LSD is a powerful hallucinogenic, which distorts the user's reality affecting time, movement and visualization. Known as a trip, LSD is sold in the form of small tabs of paper impregnated with the drug so it can be swallowed. The appearance of the paper tabs varies depending on the supplier, and they can carry a multitude of potential logos similar to ecstasy tablets. Street names include tab, trips, blotter, Lucy, paper mushrooms and liquid acid.

Magic Mushrooms
'Magic mushroom' is the slang name given to naturally grown hallucinogenic fungus, typically the liberty cap or the fly agaric mushroom. The sensation is similar to the effects of taking LSD. Other slang names include shrooms, mushies, magic and liberties.

Methamphetamine
The strongest and most harmful type of amphetamine, this drug is more commonly known as crystal meth. It can come in the form of crystals, powder or tablets, and can be swallowed, snorted, smoked or injected. The effects are described as similar to cocaine, with similar side effects including paranoia, agitation and aggression. Street names include ice, glass, Christine, meth and crank.

CLASS B DRUGS

Possession of Class B drugs can result in up to five years in prison and/or an unlimited fine. The supply and production of Class B drugs carries a prison sentence of up to fourteen years and/or an unlimited fine.

Amphetamines
More commonly known as speed, amphetamines cause users to feel energized and over-stimulated. A popular drug on the clubbing scene, amphetamine was once also used in the production of certain slimming tablets because it boosted the metabolism, which resulted in loss of appetite. It comes in the form of a thick powder with a claggy consistency, and is white with a pinkish or yellow tinge.

Barbiturates
Barbiturates provide a feeling of intoxication and relaxation. They are one of the ingredients in the lethal injection used for capital punishment. They are used in controlled doses for the treatment of migraines and epilepsy and as a general anaesthesia. Street names include barbs, downers, goofballs and sleepers.

Cannabis
Cannabis is one of the most widely used drugs in the UK; it can be easily recognized by its distinctive, pungent smell. Tetrahydrocannabinol (THC) is the chemical found in cannabis, which causes the user to feel relaxed and happy. It is popular with people suffering from chronic pain conditions, as the relaxing effect offers the sufferer a great deal of pain relief.

Cannabis plants.

Cannabis plants are used to create many different forms of the drug and can come in different strengths, 'skunk' being the strongest. The resin of the plant is compacted into black or dark brown blocks, known as hash. The dried leaves and flowering bush of the female plant are known as grass or weed. The sticky substance derived from the plant is known as cannabis oil, but is not in such common abundance as the resin or leaves. Cannabis can be smoked

Flowering cannabis bush.

Dried cannabis bush.

in a hand-rolled cigarette known as a joint or a spliff, and it can also be consumed as a drink or foodstuff.

Indigenous to central Asia and India, cannabis is successfully grown in the UK by emulating the growing conditions in those countries, using a purpose-made irrigation system, high-voltage heat lights, fans and ventilation: such a set-up is known as a farm or a grow. I have attended countless cannabis farms. They can be

Ventilation familiar at cannabis farms.

hazardous scenes to work in, as the electricity supply has generally been bypassed, so needs making safe by the electricity board: this involves disconnecting the electricity, so you then have to work in the dark until the window coverings can be removed.

The smell is incredibly pungent and it can linger on hair and clothing. I can recall one occasion when I was called to the local shop after working in a cannabis farm for several hours. I had got used to the smell and didn't realize how bad it was until I received a few surprised looks and was given a wide berth from my fellow shoppers.

There is a lot of controversy surrounding the classification of cannabis as a Class B drug. In 2004 it was reclassified as a Class C drug, meaning it was considered less harmful. But following political debate, in 2009 it was reinstated to a Class B drug, although the debate regarding its use continues to rage on.

Cannabis has many slang names, including weed, skunk, pot, marijuana, grass, ganja, hashish, dope, bud and herb.

Synthetic Highs

Formerly known as 'legal highs' before they were made illegal in May 2016, these drugs are packaged as a smoking mixture and consist of various chemicals that simulate the effects of cocaine and cannabis. These drugs gathered notoriety after their usage was widely reported in prison. Their popularity is in part due to the fact that traces of the drug consist of a chemical compound, which does not currently show up on mandatory drug tests.

Synthetic highs are potentially lethal, and have indeed caused many deaths since their production. The chemical composition of the high has caused people to hallucinate, act with extreme levels of violence and become psychologically unstable.

Typically they come packaged in small paper or foil packets and are currently sold under a number of street names, most commonly spice, black mamba, clockwork orange, Amsterdam gold, Bombay blue and annihilation. Liquid spice can be vaped using an e-cigarette, or sprayed on paper that is then cut up, added to a roll-up and smoked.

Ketamine

Originally intended as a general anaesthetic, and in particular a horse tranquillizer, ketamine has become popular as a recreational drug by people craving the effects of the floating sensation and intense relaxation concomitant with anaesthesia, which includes not being able to move and a sensation of being detached from the body. This drug can also cause hallucinations, known as trips.

Ketamine comes in liquid form when used for its original intention as an anaesthetic by the medical profession. On the street it is available as a tablet or in powder form, so it can be swallowed or snorted. Slang names include donkey dust, ket, vitamin K and Special K.

CLASS C DRUGS

Possession of Class C drugs can result in up to two years in prison and/or an unlimited fine. The supply and production of Class C drugs carries a prison sentence up to fourteen years and/or an unlimited fine.

Anabolic Steroids
Whilst anabolic steroids are included as a Class C drug, it is not an offence for an individual to possess them for personal use, when provided by a pharmacist with a doctor's prescription.

Tranquillizers
Used as a muscle relaxant or sedative to allow periods of calm, or as a cure for insomnia, tranquillizers such as Rohypnol (also known as the 'date rape drug'), Diazepam and Temazepam are usually given out by doctors on prescription; however, they can also be obtained illegally as a street drug. They are sometimes taken by users to 'come down' after binges of cocaine, speed or ecstasy.

Gammahydroxybutyrate (GHB)
The full chemical name for this drug certainly makes us appreciate the acronym! GHB acts as a strong sedative that relaxes the body and lowers inhibitions. It comes in liquid form, and is also known as liquid ecstasy.

PSYCHOACTIVE SUBSTANCES

Any new drugs that come available can be subject to a one year banning order, until such time as the effects can be analysed and the government is able to classify them, depending on the harm they can cause.

Police can issue a penalty to any person being in possession of a substance that is classed as psychoactive: that is, categorized by its ability to produce hallucinations, alter perception of time and space, cause drowsiness, or alter levels of alertness.

A popular example of a substance that is classified as psychoactive is nitrous oxide. Also known as laughing gas or hippie crack, it can make the user feel dizzy, giddy and euphoric. It has gained popularity as a party drug, and is often found in small, silver pressurized containers.

Solvents and alcohol are also classed as drugs, as they can alter a person's state of mind, be easily abused and are also highly addictive. Some addicts are able to sustain a normal lifestyle whilst maintaining their addiction – the functioning alcoholic who is still able to get up, go to work and be productive is a typical example. However, research has shown that prolonged abuse and the excessive consumption of any intoxicating substance can be detrimental to the user's long-term physical and mental health, and sometimes the effects can be irreversible.

SIGNS OF DRUG USE

When drug use or drug dealing has taken place in a crime scene, experienced crime scene investigators and police officers will quickly recognize the signs. When an entire house has been used as a purpose-built farm for the production of cannabis, typically there will be circular air vents threaded through purpose-made holes in walls and ceilings, and tarpaulins covering windows and doors to deter prying eyes and to keep the heat in.

Plant pots of various sizes will be in abundance, as will large quantities of soil and fertilizer. The bath will be kept full of water, as will waterbutts or buckets. There will be transformers lining the room to enable a mass supply of electricity to all the bulbs and electric fans, and wall charts that record plant growth, and also thermometers. There will usually be plenty of air fresheners throughout the house too, in a keen attempt to conceal the distinctive odour.

Depending on other types of drug use, such crime scenes will be full of needles, alcohol wipes, citric acid or Jif lemon juice, possibly a sharps bin, scales, snap bags, tinfoil, blackened spoons, cigarette lighters, plastic pop bottles with holes cut in and signs of smoke, mirrors, residue from powder lines, razor blades, cigarette papers and filters, tourniquets, wraps or pieces of plastic that have been twisted, clingfilm and powder. It is also more than likely that if the people in the scene are caught in the act, they may be in possession of a lot of cash and a number of mobile phones.

A number of drug-testing kits are available in the custody office at police stations, such as the Marquis Reagent Kit, which can be used to test drugs on a prisoner once they have stated what the

Tinfoil and blackened spoons are a sign of drug use.

drug is, and if it is for personal use. The kit will change a particular colour depending on what the drug is, for example heroin or amphetamine. If police stop a driver whom they believe is under the influence of alcohol they can perform a road-side breath test using a breathalyser. There is also a piece of equipment called the Drager drug test that can be used for road-side testing for drugs: this measures a sample of oral fluid to indicate if the driver is under the influence of drugs.

TOXICOLOGY

Overdoses are very common in drug users and can lead to irreversible health problems or even death. It may not necessarily be due to having too much of a particular drug, but part of the risk is not knowing how pure (strong) it is, or what it is cut (mixed) with. Particularly when drugs are in a powder form they can be cut with anything from sugar, powdered milk, paracetamol, nutmeg or dirt, so it might be that the overdose is due to the toxicity of the mix of drugs. For example, even something as innocuous and innocent as the nutmeg, if taken intravenously, can prove fatal.

A toxin can be classed as a poison that causes a response from the immune system. If the toxin is too strong for the immune system to fight, then this can result in death. Over-consumption of even the most bizarre substances can also result in death – there are reported cases of people who have died after consuming too many litres of Coca Cola. Even something as pure as water can result in poisoning if too much is consumed over a short space of time: this occurs because the brain functions become fatally disturbed by the imbalance of electrolytes, as the water floods the system, ridding it of much needed substances such as sodium.

Toxicology is the science of investigating the effects of drugs and poisons. Toxicologists are not just concerned with fatalities: they are also involved in analysing samples in relation to drink or drug driving offences. Chapter 2 describes the process of a post mortem and how a number of samples are taken, which can then be submitted to a toxicologist for further investigation. Hair is also used by toxicologists to determine long-term drug abuse.

If toxicology results are an essential part of your storyline, then please be aware that the time it takes to examine the toxicology samples, and for the results to be returned to the SIO, can take several weeks and in certain cases even months, depending on the nature of the case and regardless of the fact it is a murder investigation. As with the systematic, painstaking examination of a crime scene, these things take as long as they take and can't be rushed.

There are many variables for the toxicologist to consider when analysing samples, particularly when fatalities have occurred. Relevant to their investigations in this respect is a toxicological term known as bioavailability, which is concerned with the absorption and measurement of a substance once it is consumed. For example, if a patient is administered morphine intravenously, then its bioavailability will be 100 per cent; however, if it is administered orally, this percentage will most likely decrease, depending on the individual's metabolic rate and factors affecting absorption.

During the investigation into Harold Shipman, who caused the death of his patients by administering fatal doses of diamorphine (heroin), several of his victims' bodies were exhumed so that toxicological samples could be taken. Reports indicated that diamorphine was present in various organs – diamorphine is relatively stable and will sustain a high level of decomposition. In this case the bioavailability of the drug indicated that it had been administered and consumed to a particular percentage.

However, given a different scenario, a user could intravenously administer heroin, yet no traces of the drug might be found in the system post mortem. The bioavailability of the administration of the drug would be 100 per cent, but if death was instantaneous, the traces of heroin would be zero because it would never have reached the point of being circulated in the blood and therefore absorption would be zero. We could further this scenario by suggesting that the drug was not self-administered but injected by a third party – you can see how this would cause complications when investigating a potential murder/manslaughter.

Other variables that the toxicologist needs to consider include the individual's age, weight and lifestyle, their ongoing exposure to the toxin, the method of administration and their state of health, including any ongoing medical conditions and medication that they may be on. Whilst certain medications or toxins may not be dangerous per se, when mixed with other substances the combination can prove fatal.

Stepping Hill Hospital in Stockport was the subject of a lengthy investigation by Greater Manchester Police, beginning in 2011. A nurse on the ward noticed that a number of patients began displaying signs of low blood sugar, although this was not in keeping with their medical complaints or their history. An initial investigation revealed that a number of saline drips and ampoules had been tampered with and contained traces of insulin, which would explain the unpredictable change in blood sugar levels. Following complications that can arise with hypoglycaemia, some patients who had been exposed to the contaminated drip died, although they did have other serious ongoing medical conditions, including in one case cancer. The job of the toxicologist was to ascertain the most likely cause of death and to what extent this could be attributed to the contaminated saline drip.

An initial arrest that was made in the course of the investigation was subsequently retracted in September 2011. Then in January 2012, another death that had occurred several days earlier was submitted to the investigation; police enquiries continued and resulted in the arrest of Victorino Chua, a nurse at the hospital.

In May 2015 Chua was convicted of two counts of murder, twenty-one counts of grievous bodily harm with intent by poisoning, and eight counts of illegally administering, or causing to be taken, a poison or noxious substance with intent to injure. He was sentenced to life imprisonment and ordered to serve a minimum of thirty-five years.

DRUGS AND CHARACTERIZATION

Drugs are very much a lifestyle choice, and it is important to portray the right addiction to the right character, just as you would make sure to describe them wearing the right kind of footwear. For example, your high-flying business executive is more likely to be using cocaine for the energy and confidence boost it provides, rather than going for the relaxing, zombie effect of heroin.

It is often said that the two motives for murder are love and money. However, I hope this chapter has provided enough information to prove that addiction can be a powerful motivator, and one that will drive your characters to commit the most heinous of crimes. Also, just think about how desperately those same characters might want to keep their addiction a secret. Owing money, blackmail and violence tend to be three scenarios that go hand in hand with people involved in the vicious cycle of drug addiction.

CHAPTER 10

Firearms

Firearms offences can include actual shootings, or scenarios where weapons are brandished during an armed robbery. Tabloid reports often concentrate on the number of incidents that occur in certain areas of a city, rather than the number of criminals and firearms that police have taken off the streets – though Greater Manchester Police, for example, has instigated a successful gun amnesty. Furthermore gun crime is not restricted to large cities: due to the availability of guns and the criminals' ability to access them, firearms incidents can happen anywhere.

This chapter will describe the firearms and ammunition typically used, and will look at how gunshot residue can be used as trace evidence. We will also discuss how shooting scenes have been inaccurately portrayed, so that in your writing you avoid the same pitfalls and ensure that your dramatic firearms incident remains plausible.

FIREARMS CLASSIFICATION

For ease of reference I shall categorize firearms as handguns, shotguns and rifles, and of course the types of ammunition used in each one. But first we need to look at what actually classifies a firearm, and may be well advised to consider the Home Office definition:

> Firearm means a lethal barrelled weapon of any description from which any shot, bullet or other missile can be discharged.
> Home Office, *Guide on Firearms Licensing Law*, April 2016

So, any relic or object that is manipulated or converted in such a manner is classed as a firearm.

Ammunition

Handguns and rifles all fire rounds, the name given to a bulleted cartridge, consisting of an outer cartridge case, percussion cap, bullet and propellant. Bullets are typically made of metal, although some police forces use rubber or plastic bullets with the intention of causing injury rather than death. The metal used may be copper, tin or lead, or sometimes a combination of all three. A bullet is categorized by its calibre, which is actually the diameter of the bullet, and is the part of the round that is discharged from a firearm.

The cartridge case contains all the components of the round. The propellant is packed behind the bullet and is what causes the 'burning' of the discharge process. Typically considered to be gunpowder, the propellant is a mixture of chemicals such as nitrocellulose, intended to produce a high volume of hot gas, also known as a charge.

The primer is located in the percussion cap or primer cup at the base of the cartridge. This is the area of the round that is struck by the firing pin causing a mixture of chemicals to explode, subsequently resulting in the ignition of the propellant. The base of the cartridge case may be marked with a head stamp, which provides information such as the manufacturer, the year of manufacture and the calibre.

Airguns

Before we look at the different types of firearm it is worth being aware of the use and availability of airguns. These are also often referred to by the name of the projectile they expel, namely pellet gun or BB (ball bearing) gun. They are used for sport and recreation, and although not illegal, regulations regarding their usage are stipulated in the Violent Crime Reduction (VCR) Act 2006, with various conditions including the location of use and the age of the user.

To anyone other than experienced firearms experts, some airguns look like real firearms, and it is not uncommon for offenders to use them during robberies and other violent crimes – so it is understandable that they are monitored under the Violent Crime Reduction Act. A BB gun is pictured opposite – just imagine if this was aimed at you by someone wearing gloves and a balaclava, and screaming at you in a threatening manner: would you know the difference?

HANDGUNS

For the sake of simplicity I shall classify handguns as being either pistols or revolvers. Firearms experts will be disapproving of the fact that I am choosing not to differentiate between single-shot, self-loading and revolving pistols, but this is a book for crime writers, so I am going to mention the different firing abilities. Pistols and revolvers are two types of handgun, which, as the name suggests, are intended to be held and supported with the hands – as opposed to the shotgun and the rifle, which rely on the body's support to maintain their stability when firing.

Pistols

A pistol is a handgun with a short barrel, designed to fire bullets at a relatively short distance, up to approximately fifty metres. Certain pistols can be considered relics, in particular the single-barrelled type with the bulbous, crescent moon-shaped handle and prominent trigger used in historic dramas during duels. That said, all firearms should be treated with respect, because they are all essentially designed to discharge a bullet, and capable of doing so with fatal consequences.

A pistol is typically hinged at the base of the handle, which allows the barrel to drop downwards once it is unlocked, so that the magazine can be loaded with cartridges. The barrel of a pistol is rifled and can be used to fire a single bullet, or it can be self-loading, which means that a number of cartridges can be loaded into the magazine and will be deployed as the magazine spring moves them into position in the barrel, ready for firing.

A single-shot pistol requires the round to be manually loaded and

A black BB gun.

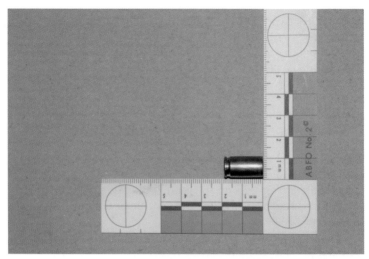

9mm cartridge case.

Base of a 9mm
cartridge case.

unloaded after it has been fired. However, there are also self-loading pistols that are designed to be loaded with a magazine of rounds, which can then be fired simultaneously. These are usually referred to as semi-automatic, and are understandably a popular choice of firearm because of the firing efficiency. The number of rounds a self-loading pistol can hold varies according to the particular make of firearm; in the majority of makes the cartridge case is expelled once each round is fired.

Revolvers

Think about a traditional Western cowboy movie from the seventies and you will be able to picture the revolver. Children of the seventies and eighties will probably remember cap guns – toy guns that you could load with rolled paper with primer sandwiched in the middle, or with plastic cap rings. When the cap of the gun hit the primer it would make a banging sound and release a smell of sulphur dioxide, just like the smell of burning matches.

Like a pistol, a revolver has a short, rifled barrel but the rounds are stored in a cylindrical chamber, as opposed to the vertical stack of the magazine that is slotted into a pistol. Most revolvers have six chambers, so the user can fire six rounds before needing to reload. There are other types of revolver with five or up to nine chambers, but this depends on the calibre – the term used to describe the diameter of the barrel.

A double-action revolver is designed to fire all rounds with each trigger pull, as the round is spun by the trigger and positioned in the firing chamber. This makes the revolver a much more efficient firearm than the single-action revolver, which has to be manually re-cocked for each shot. I have already mentioned that a self-loading pistol will typically discharge the cartridge case, whereas in the case of a revolver, the cartridge cases are usually retained within the cylinder. This is relevant because, as we will see later, the cartridge case can provide a valuable source of forensic evidence, as well as help identify the firearm used.

RIFLES

Known as a long gun, a rifle can typically be described as an elongated pistol that is designed to fire from the shoulder – it can be either single- or double-barrelled, and in both the barrel will be 'rifled', which we will discuss in more detail later on. Typically they are used for hunting or during warfare due to their accuracy and greater field of fire. The calibre and type of rifle determines how powerful it is. Like the single-shot pistol, the single-shot rifle is hinged so that the barrel can be swung downwards and loaded. Rifles can also be bolt action or self-loading.

SHOTGUNS

Also classed as a long gun, a shotgun is designed to be fired from the shoulder. The main distinctions between a shotgun and other forms of firearm are the ammunition and the barrel. A shotgun does not fire rounds; it fires shot (hence the name), which we will look at in more detail later. The other important distinction is the barrel, which is smooth bore and not rifled.

Shotguns can be single-barrelled or, most typically, double-barrelled. They can be self-loading, pump-action or semi-automatic, and can be adapted to become the cliché bank robber's weapon of choice, the sawn-off shotgun. The end of the shotgun barrel may be muzzled, also known as being choked: this involves decreasing the diameter at the end of the barrel so the distribution of the fired shot is more condensed, rather than widely spread.

Shot

Shotgun cartridges are typically plastic, although some paper cases are also manufactured. The base of the cartridge is usually brass, which, having been fired, just like a cartridge case, may be scarred by the extractor marks of the shotgun as well as bearing a manufacturer's head stamp. Whereas a bulleted cartridge is rounded, the front of a shotgun cartridge is flattened.

Typically shot consists of small rounds of lead, packed in the front of the cartridge and then compacted with wadding – circular discs made of card or felt that cause a seal between the projectile and the shot. A smokeless powder acts as the propellant and is packed against the other side of the wadding. A priming mixture is also added, which will initiate the necessary chemical reaction (once ignited by firing the priming cup) to cause the burning and discharge process.

RIFLING

With the exception of shotguns, all the other categories of firearm we have discussed so far have one thing in common: their barrels are rifled. This term refers to the spiralling indentation cut into the inside of the barrel, its purpose being to stabilize the bullet and maintain its accuracy once it is spun through the barrel.

The depressions cut into the interior surface of the barrel are known as lands and grooves: the grooves refer to the portion that is carved away, and the lands are the untouched sections that stand proud. The striation marks inside each barrel can be as unique as fingerprints, because the metal used in the manufacture of firearms is so hard that the cutting tool itself will change whilst it is carving the groove in the barrel, resulting in a unique carving pattern.

When the round is fired the unique striation marks will indent the bullet, providing investigators with the opportunity to later match the bullet back to the firearm it was discharged from. Not only will the bullet be scarred with striation marks in the last few centimetres as it exits the firearm, the rest of the round (namely the cartridge) also provides us with forensic opportunities because of the indentation from the firing pin, ejector or extractor and the breech face marks. The weight and dimensions of a spent bullet can indicate the calibre of the cartridge it has been discharged from, so experts know which type of firearm has been used.

THE POSSESSION OF FIREARMS

Whereas the United States of America is notorious for gun crime and the constitutional right to bear arms, Britain is known for its efforts to install legal controls over the public's access to firearms. Although many criminals still manage to obtain various forms of firearm illegally, and other potentially fatal items such as Tasers and grenades, licensing laws control the usage of rifles and shotguns for sporting purposes, and since 1996, handguns have been classed as illegal. One event in particular led to this ban on handgun ownership: the Dunblane massacre.

On 13 March 1996 Thomas Hamilton, aged forty-three, drove to Dunblane Primary School armed with four legally owned handguns – two pistols and two revolvers. He then set out on a shooting spree that tragically took the lives of sixteen small children and their teacher; a further fifteen people were injured before Hamilton

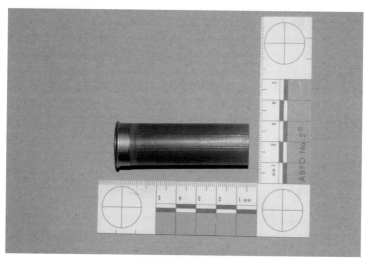

Shotgun cartridge.

Base of a shotgun
cartridge case.

fatally shot himself. The attack was believed to have lasted less than five minutes.

The Dunblane tragedy followed a massacre ten years before, in 1987, in Hungerford in Berkshire, when Michael Ryan armed himself with a handgun and two semi-automatic rifles. Ryan's spree consisted of random shootings throughout Hungerford, concluding with his suicide by shooting himself in the head. During his rampage, Ryan killed fifteen people, including his own mother, and injured a further fifteen. There is no known motive for Ryan's attack although it is suspected he was possibly suffering with schizophrenia or psychosis. At the time of the attack he was in legal possession of seven licensed firearms.

After the Dunblane massacre and the horrific events in Hungerford, an enquiry conducted by the Honourable Lord Cullen called for tighter gun controls on the private ownership of handguns. These calls were backed up by the parents of Dunblane, who initiated the Snowdrop petition, a campaign calling for a total ban on handgun ownership. As a result, the Firearms (Amendment No. 2) Act 1997 was passed, which banned the private ownership of all cartridge ammunition handguns, even those that had previously been classified as small-calibre pistols.

Since the 1997 amendment, such mass shootings have thankfully not been repeated – with the exception of a massacre in Cumbria in June 2010, when Derrick Bird, a fifty-two-year-old taxi driver, committed a two-hour killing spree that took the lives of twelve people and injured a further eleven. Bird then committed suicide, shooting himself with his own rifle. Bird had been a licensed gun holder for twenty years, and the two weapons he used, the rifle and shotgun, were legally held by him.

Unfortunately, gun crime continues to be a major problem for police forces across the United Kingdom, as criminals continue to access and distribute illegally owned firearms. Drugs and the ongoing gang culture that dominates many towns and cities are predominantly responsible for the continued supply and demand of firearms and ammunition. However, it is perhaps worth noting that in July 2014 Greater Manchester Police held a gun amnesty, when people were given the opportunity to hand over their firearms without fear of prosecution; 225 firearms and over 3,500 rounds of ammunition were surrendered. Then in April 2016, GMP held another two-week gun amnesty, when a total of 221 firearms were handed in, and thousands of rounds of ammunition.

These figures give an indication as to just how many firearms are available on Britain's streets. So if it is part of your storyline for your character to have access to a firearm, then there is no need to worry about whether this is a plausible scenario.

ACCIDENTAL DISCHARGE OF A FIREARM

Accidentally causing a weapon to discharge is a common form of defence in many cases concerning shooting incidents – after all, accidents do happen. In America in 2015, 265 children under the age of eighteen accidentally discharged a firearm, resulting in eighty-five fatalities. And it is not just children who can be accidentally trigger happy: reports of adults mistakenly shooting themselves in the foot, hand and even buttocks are not the work of fiction but are surprisingly common, particularly when the aforementioned gang members are posing in front of the mirror with the firearm they have been asked to hide.

The potential storyline 'I dropped the gun and it went off, Your Honour' is in fact not acceptable, and nor is the claim that the trigger was pulled in error: ballistic experts will conduct a number of tests to support or refute these theories, and will also look at the external ballistics, which are concerned with the process of trajectory, therefore providing an indication as to the direction and flight pattern of the projectile.

Before any forensic examination of a firearm takes place, it is first made safe to handle by a firearms expert. Observations will be made as to whether or not the weapon is cocked, if the safety catch is on, if the firearm is loaded, the number of cartridges, and whether they are primed and ready to fire. The make and model will also be recorded, including any details of serial numbers – criminals usually file these off to avoid detection, or when reconditioning firearms, but it is still possible to recover the original serial number using a technique known as metallographic etching.

When considering the possibility of accidental discharge, the many potential scenarios can be categorized as follows:

Faulty lock mechanism: The lock mechanism holds the firing mechanism in place until the trigger is pulled. A fault in the lock mechanism will ultimately result in the weapon firing.

Faulty safety mechanism: The safety mechanism has either failed or has not been correctly applied. Tests can be conducted to ascertain if there is a genuine malfunction.

Trigger misuse: This can include low trigger pressure, where the trigger pressure is set to as light as 1lb (hair trigger) and is subsequently more easily discharged than a firearm that relies on the average 5lb trigger pressure. Part of the examination will determine the amount of pressure needed to activate that particular firearm, and this will help with claims that the trigger accidentally fired while being snatched out of a hand or snagged on an item of clothing.

Dropped firearm: Where it is claimed that a firearm has been 'dropped', a number of tests can be conducted to test this claim. The firearm will be subject to a replication of the alleged jarring by being subjected to a series of controlled impacts. Although possible, it is an unlikely cause of accidental discharge.

The National Ballistics Intelligence Service (NABIS) was formed in 2008, and provides intelligence that can link gun crimes, specialist ballistics advice, the capability to test fire weapons and a database of firearms and ammunition. There are four regional forensic hubs located in four police forces: Greater Manchester, West Midlands, Glasgow and the Metropolitan Police.

THE OSCAR PISTORIUS CASE

Oscar Pistorius is famous for more than just his success as a Paralympic athlete and as a participant at the 2012 Olympics: he found notoriety off the running track following the fatal shooting of his girlfriend, Reeva Steenkamp, in 2013. In the early hours of St Valentine's Day, it is alleged that Pistorius thought there was an intruder in the toilet and fired four shots from his semi-automatic pistol through the toilet door. He did not deny shooting the gun, but claimed it was an act of self-defence. It transpired that there was no intruder, but in fact it was Reeva in the toilet – she had been shot three times.

One of the reasons the trial received so much publicity was not just the circumstances surrounding the killing of a well-known model by a sports celebrity, but also the fact that the judge ruled that the case, which was heard in the High Court of South Africa, could be broadcast live, attracting even more media attention. The focus of the trial involved the veracity behind Pistorius' intruder claim, and also whether or not he was wearing his prosthetic legs at the time of the shooting and afterwards.

Pistorius claimed he had been wearing his prosthetic legs when attempting to beat the locked toilet door open with a cricket bat, but the prosecution claimed otherwise, supported by the findings of a forensic expert and ballistics analyst. The forensic expert refuted Pistorius' claim because the damage to the door was too low; likewise the ballistics expert concluded that when Pistorius fired the four shots, his gun was at a level that coincided with him being stood on his stumps; this also coincided with the angle of the bullets, which were centred just below the door handle.

Pistorius claimed that he thought Reeva was in bed next to him at the time of the suspected intrusion and even claimed that he had spoken to her beforehand. He was originally sentenced to culpable homicide (manslaughter) in 2014, but the Court of Appeal overturned this decision in 2015 and instead he was found guilty of murder and sentenced to six years in August 2016.

GUN-SHOT RESIDUE (GSR) AND OTHER FORENSIC OPPORTUNITIES

Being able to identify firearms and ammunition through the NABIS database is an invaluable resource and provides a wealth of intelligence for investigators. The individual characteristics caused during the discharge phase of the internal ballistics are unique, and provide very strong evidential value. There is also the opportunity to obtain further trace evidence, fingerprints and DNA from recovered firearms and ammunition.

Gun-shot residue (GSR) is the by-product of a discharged firearm, and is caused as a result of the high velocity combined with a release of gases, traces of propellant, soot and burnt primer. The distribution of GSR on a person can indicate whether or not they fired the weapon, or were left holding it afterwards. GSR is distributed differently depending on the type of firearm – firing a handgun is different from the shoulder brace employed when firing a rifle or shotgun, but regardless of this, firearms residue will still be deposited on the firer.

GSR is collected from suspects by swabbing their hands, face and neck, and by taking nail scrapings. Consideration will also be given to the recovery of gloves and balaclavas that may have been worn at the time of the offence. Various factors will affect the persistence of GSR, as with any other trace evidence, but tests indicate that it can be retained on skin for between three and four hours after the weapon has been discharged, but may be retained longer on clothing and other items.

The blackening caused by GSR is often found on the entry wound of a firearms victim, and can be used to estimate the firing range. The angle of entry can also provide valuable information in piecing together the sequence of events. The calibre, type of ammunition and the proximity of the gun when fired will all impact on the amount of damage caused to the victim. I have seen an entry wound on the side of a victim's chest that looked so small and innocuous; it seemed hardly likely that it had resulted in their death. Other than this small hole there wasn't a single mark on the body. However, the post mortem revealed just how much damage had been caused to the major organs when the bullet ripped through the body.

Shotgun injuries are different again, and depending on the range from which the gun is fired and the dispersal of the shot, it is possible to rip a person's chest open or obliterate their face; it is likely that damage caused by a shotgun will not be as 'neat' as damage caused by a bullet.

If a firearm is pressed directly against the victim's skin when it is fired, then the residue will be forced inside the wound, following the track of the bullet and leaving few traces on the body, and possibly giving the impression that it is an exit, rather than an entry wound (assuming that the exit wound is a more precise hole, although this is not always the case). It is always beneficial to have a ballistics expert present during the post mortem of a firearms victim, as they can help determine any damage caused to the bullet if, for example, it has ricocheted off bones, etc.

In such cases where a firearm is discharged in close proximity to the victim, it is also highly likely that traces of the victim's blood will be found on the weapon or in the barrel, which is obviously going to present a positive link to the crime scene. In the two cases described below, this fact, and the position of the firearms at the crime scene, led investigators to convict the individuals who were guilty of murder.

In the first case, five family members were fatally shot at their home, White House Farm, in Essex in August 1985. The person who reported the shooting was the son, twenty-four-year old Jeremy Bamber. The victims included his adoptive parents, his sister Sheila and her six-year-old twin boys. Bamber told the police that his father had rung him saying his sister had gone berserk with a gun.

The police made their way to the scene, where they discovered the bodies of Nevill Bamber in the kitchen, his wife June on the floor in the master bedroom, next to her daughter Sheila. The twins had been shot while asleep in their beds. The scene was secure when police arrived, with the back door locked from the inside. Twenty-five shots had been fired in total and mostly at close range.

Bamber strongly insinuated to the police that his sister's well-documented history of schizophrenia was most likely to have led to the murder suicide scene. Allegedly there had been a discussion that evening, suggesting that Sheila should consider arranging foster care for the children. Initially the case seemed cut and dried, leaving Bamber a very rich man, as he was the sole inheritor. However, there were a number of discrepancies at the time of the crime scene investigation. First, a silencer belonging to the semi-automatic rifle that was used to commit the murders was found in a cupboard several days after the shooting. The silencer bore flecks of paint and also blood, which matched Sheila's. Scientists were able to match the paint to some damage on the mantelpiece above the Aga in the kitchen, where it appeared Nevill Bamber had put up a fight prior to being shot dead: at some point the silencer had come into contact with the mantelpiece more than just the once, resulting in the paint transfer.

It did not seem feasible that Sheila had committed the murders, shot herself twice in the throat, removed the silencer, placed it back in the cupboard and then made her way back upstairs where she lay with the firearm resting on her body pointing towards her neck as she died. Tests proved that had the silencer been attached to the weapon, Sheila would not have managed to shoot herself, as she would have been unable to reach the trigger. Surely, if this had been the case, she would have removed the silencer and just left it next to her – why, after murdering her parents and two children would she then have felt compelled to tidy it away?

To further strengthen the case that Sheila was not the killer, firearms experts also commented on how clean her hands and nightdress were. Had she fired the twenty-five shots, then the rifle would have needed reloading twice, a process that would have left traces of lead and gun oil on her hands and clothing.

Suspicion quickly turned to Bamber as this new evidence came to light, and he was found guilty of five counts of murder in October 1986; his subsequent appeals were dismissed.

A case that bears chilling similarities to the White House Farm murders is the murder of Robert and Patricia Seddon at their home in Sale, Greater Manchester on 4 July 2012. The couple were murdered by their son, Stephen, who was motivated by the prospect of inheriting their money once they were dead. Seddon had a record for burglary and petty theft, and had been sentenced to a year in prison in 2000 for fraud offences. When he realized his parents had named each other as beneficiaries in their will, and himself as sole heir were they both to die, Seddon began plotting their demise.

In March 2012 he announced that he was taking his parents and nephew (who had lived with the Seddons since his mother's death) out for the day. However, Seddon allegedly lost control of the car, causing it to plunge into the canal. Seddon managed to free himself, and it seemed that his three passengers were about to drown. Eyewitnesses described how they saw him jumping on the roof of the submerging vehicle, until their arrival prompted him to change tactic and rescue them.

It later transpired that Seddon's father had confided in his GP that he believed his son wanted to kill him and he was going to challenge him about the canal incident after discovering his son had watched a programme on how to escape from a sinking vehicle. But Seddon murdered his parents the following day after arriving at their house with a sawn-off shotgun. He shot his mother in the head in the hallway and his father in the neck as he tried to get up off the sofa. He then positioned the firearm in his father's lap with his right hand on the gun in an attempt to stage a murder suicide scenario.

The placing of the weapon did not fool investigators, who surmised that first, Mr Seddon would not have been able to shoot himself with a sawn-off shotgun because his arms were too short, and second, that the recoil from the shotgun would have left the deceased's body and the weapon in a completely different position, not sitting in the staged position they were found.

Seddon was found guilty of two counts of murder and attempted murder, and will hopefully never be paroled.

ARMING YOUR CHARACTERS

The White House Farm and Seddon murders highlight scenarios that are often inaccurately portrayed in fiction – always consider the size of the weapon and accessibility to the trigger. It would be inaccurate to describe a drive-by shooting where your character is wielding a shotgun or rifle given their size – it would be impossible to position such a gun on the shoulder because the car seat, head rests, steering wheel and dashboard would get in the way.

Another inaccurate scenario is a drive-by shooting where the shooter is in the passenger seat being driven past the target: even a highly-trained sniper would struggle to take aim and fire while the car is moving. Likewise with your heroic character that is described as running while they shoot – it wouldn't happen. Guns can be heavy and cumbersome, and when they are fired, the recoil can be quite powerful. Remember that some weapons need loading and reloading, so describing a scenario where a shooter stands and peppers a building or bus stop with bullets for five minutes is again inaccurate.

If a shooting scene is going to be relevant to your storyline, then unless you really know your guns, I would advise against going into too much technical detail. Also bear in mind that bullets can travel a fair distance, but the flight of a bullet can easily be knocked off course due to ricochet. As a result, spent bullets can be found in the most unlikely places and may not be completely intact, depending on the surfaces they have passed through.

Finally, remember the accuracy and range of each type of firearm – a handgun would not be used to aim at a target if the distance were greater than fifty metres. The type of firearm used may also depend upon the era in which your story is based, so additional research is always useful to ensure that the weapon matches the historic period.

CHAPTER 11

Other Forensic Practices and Agencies

This final chapter describes additional forensic practices that may add value to your crime writing as well as providing an overview of the other roles and agencies that are frequently drawn into a criminal investigation, and which may not have been already mentioned. I also hope that providing details of other forensic disciplines may be an inspiration to you, by increasing your knowledge of what forensic experts can achieve through thoughtful analysis.

Some major crimes and murders are so unprecedented that crime scene investigators and detectives are required to push their problem-solving skills to the limit when it comes to recovering evidence and obtaining the information they need to piece the facts of a case together. But where there's a will, there's always a way, and I hope this chapter provides you with an awareness of the additional forensic practices you may need to extend and enhance your storyline.

FORENSIC PRACTICES

Forensic Accountancy

Fraud is the crime of stealing thousands, if not millions of pounds from innocent victims – and without even having to pull on a balaclava. The internet has provided us with countless opportunities to make our lives easier, from doing a quick Google search to find out what the weather is going to be like, to online banking. It has also given computer-wise criminals the chance to drain our online bank accounts, and to indulge in identity theft, blackmail, tax evasion and money laundering.

All these crimes can be investigated with the assistance of a forensic accountant. If you need any convincing about how beneficial forensic accounting can be during the course of a criminal investigation, then it is worth knowing that the FBI (Federal Bureau of Investigation) and the Internal Revenue Service (IRS) were hugely instrumental in ending the reign of the infamous American gangster Al Capone, who was well known for his involvement in racketeering during Prohibition.

Handwriting and Document Analysis

Fraud and blackmail are amongst the many crimes that may involve the expertise of a handwriting and document analyst, perhaps to authenticate the signature on a cheque, contract or even a will. But sometimes, proving the authenticity of a handwritten document can have wider implications than investigating illegal financial gains.

When police discovered the body of Daniel Whitworth in a grave-yard in Barking on 20 September 2014, he was found with a suicide note that implicated himself in the death of another young man, Gabriel Kovari, who had died on 28 August 2014. It was initially considered that neither of these deaths was suspicious, and therefore did not warrant any further investigation. However, handwriting experts later examined the suicide note and were able to conclude that it had actually been written by a man named Stephen Port, with the deliberate intention of framing Whitworth for Kovari's death.

In fact Stephen Port was responsible for the death of both men, and two more besides. He had met the men on a social networking site and had arranged to meet them; he had then plied them with drinks laced with GHB (see Chapter 9), and once they were inebriated, had raped them, satisfying his own sexual gratification and fetish for having sex with young twenty-something men (known as 'Twinks') while they were unconscious. Obviously, their unconscious state did not allow them to consent so Port's fetish can only ever be classified as rape. It is believed they died because of an overdose of drugs he gave them like GHB and the possible added cocktail of Viagra, poppers and meow meow. Despite the fact that the bodies of Kovari, Whitworth and a third man, Jack Taylor, were all discovered in the same location, investigations originally concluded that the deaths were not suspicious.

Port has been served a life sentence for killing the four men, as well as for rape, and administering a substance with intent. At the time of writing, the Independent Police Complaints Commission (IPCC) are looking into the suggestion that police failed to link the deaths and recognize the suspicious circumstances – but whatever the outcome, the handwriting analysis of the 'suicide note' played a crucial part in the police investigation.

Graffiti

Handwriting analysis isn't restricted to traditional pen and paper: experts will also investigate the work of graffiti artists, who use

Graffiti tag on a railway bridge.

spray paint to produce their works of art and leave their tags. Graffiti is a common problem at railways and tube stations, because by leaving their tags in such busy locations or even on train carriages, artists hope that their 'work' will be seen by as many people as possible. The cost to the rail companies and the Underground service of cleaning it all up amounts to millions every year, not to mention the policing aspect as vandals access high-risk areas to leave their mark.

The East Lancashire Railway is a stretch of heritage railway based in Bury, Greater Manchester. Because of its authentic station and trains it is popular with enthusiasts, and has also been used as a popular filming location. Years ago I was asked to attend there with the British Transport Police after a number of carriages and part of the railway had been used as a canvas. I was asked to photographically record the spray-painted tags, which were then produced in an album and later used as evidence, which led to the successful prosecution of the offenders. The British Transport Police now has a database for storing the tags of graffiti artists, and this helps in their prosecution, in conjunction with the services of a handwriting analyst.

Forensic Linguistics
This discipline involves the investigation of the written or spoken word. Examples of when it could be used include analysing black-

mail, death threats and even text messages, to determine whether the suspect was indeed the author of such a text, or whether it was sent by someone else in an attempt to evade detection or implicate others.

The murder of fifteen-year-old Danielle Jones is one of those tragic cases where the body has never been found, but all the evidence suggests that murder has taken place. Danielle went missing near her home in Essex on 18 June 2001. Her uncle, Stuart Campbell, was sentenced to a minimum of twenty years on suspicion of her abduction and murder. All the evidence weighed against him as being responsible for Danielle's death; in particular, evidence was provided by a linguistics expert who analysed text messages on Campbell's phone, which had allegedly been sent by Danielle.

The text messages in question were typed in capital letters, whereas Danielle was known to type hers using lower case. In addition, another text had abbreviated the word 'what' to 'wot', whereas Danielle always used the text abbreviation 'wat'. Inconsistencies such as these may seem insignificant out of context, but as evidence in a murder enquiry, the work of the linguistics expert can be conclusive.

Linguistics analysts can also prove invaluable when analysing speech. This can be useful when voice recognition is required to examine recorded bomb threats, ransom requests, death threats or obscene phone calls. Perhaps the most famous case involving voice recognition is that of the character Wearside Jack.

John Humble sent a number of hoax communications to police during 1978 and 1979 in which he claimed to be Peter Sutcliffe, also known as the Yorkshire Ripper. Humble was motivated by his hatred of the police and also by his consuming desire for attention and notoriety, and this drove him to send three letters and one audio message in which he claimed to be the Ripper. Detectives therefore moved their investigation from Yorkshire to Sunderland in an attempt to track down the man with the Wearside accent. As a direct result of this, Sutcliffe continued to attack young women over a further two-year period.

In 2000, Humble was arrested for being drunk and disorderly, and the DNA samples taken from him while in custody resulted in a hit against the DNA profile obtained from the gummed envelope in which he had sent his twisted correspondence. He was sentenced to eight years' imprisonment for perverting the course of justice.

Paper and Ink

Part of document analysis includes comparing ink samples to a suspect's pen or printer, or even the unique indentation produced through wear and tear by pens and printers. The different types can also be used for comparison purposes, and there is always the potential for recovering fingerprints from documents or DNA from the gummed area of an envelope. If paper has been torn from a pad or other source, there may be the opportunity to match this through the process of physical fit.

Stamps only became self-adhesive in 2001, so if your writing is based around or before that period, you also have the opportunity to locate your character's DNA on stamps. Also remember that technology has changed significantly over the years, and depending on your era, and before the common usage of computers and word processors, there would have been the opportunity to obtain carbon copies and typewriter reels as evidence.

If something has been written on paper or a surface that is located on top of another piece of paper – for example the next page in a notebook – then it will leave an indentation. This can be enhanced using magnetic fingerprint powders, chemical treatments or, in cases where the indentation is barely visible, an electrostatic detection apparatus (ESDA). ESDA is a non-destructive process that sends an electric charge and toner to a piece of paper in order to reveal any latent indentation. The toner is applied to the film that covers the paper, which is why it is a non-invasive procedure.

COMPUTER CRIME AND MOBILE PHONES

As computer technology continues to thrive and advance, so too does the criminal mind. While many appreciate social media, it is a scourge for others who may find themselves stalked and harassed. Chat-room users can encounter similar problems, while criminals take advantage of such sites to peddle porn. The Dark Web is renowned for providing surfers with an abundance of hard-core pornography, images of child abuse, and even acts of necrophilia and bestiality. It also provides users with the opportunity to buy drugs, firearms and counterfeit goods – basically if it is illegal, it will be on there.

Hackers are also a new breed of criminal that take full advantage of computer technology. They will either hack into the accounts of a business to steal personal information, including bank account details, or they will hold companies and organizations to ransom with the threat of a computer virus that will disable their systems unless they meet their requests. However, as much as criminals have adapted ways to abuse the internet and computer technology, forensic computer analysts are able to analyse their software and retrace their virtual footsteps.

Mobile phone technology also continues to progress, and we have moved from the archetypal mobile phone, which was the size of a house brick with its extending aerial, to smart phones and mobile phones so small they can easily be smuggled into prisons. As with computers, mobile phone usage can be traced and also tracked; triangulation (also referred to as pinging) is the process of identifying the location of a mobile phone and the areas in which it was last used. This is done by locating it to the nearest mobile phone transmitter, therefore helping police when they are searching for a missing person or retracing the movements of a murder suspect.

CCTV, FACIAL RECONSTRUCTION AND E-FIT

CCTV has become a useful tool for investigators, and also acts as a deterrent against crime. These days there are cameras everywhere, and imaging experts are able to download the footage from these cameras and reproduce them either as evidence in court, or to provide a still copy of a suspect's face. By slowing down and tracking the footage from CCTV, the experts can provide a re-enactment of a violent assault, or capture the registration plate from a suspect's vehicle.

Facial reconstruction has also been a valuable contribution to many murder investigations and missing people enquiries. As the name suggests, it is the process of reconstructing a person's face from their skeletal remains by reproducing it in a medium such as clay. Richard Neave is a renowned British expert when it comes to facial reconstruction; in particular he is known for his facial reconstruction of Lindow Man. He also reconstructed the features of the murdered fifteen-year-old Karen Price, whose case is discussed in the entomology section below.

Facial mapping may also be helpful in an investigation. This involves placing a suspect's image against a still taken from a CCTV camera or similar, and making relevant comparisons to ascertain

Video surveillance by a CCTV camera.

if the crime scene image matches that of the suspect. This is done by incorporating morphological analysis and superimposing it on to digital images, and matching any unique physiological characteristics, which may include scars or tattoos.

But what about reconstructing the image of a face without skeletal remains or a CCTV image? How can the face of a murderer or rapist be reconstructed using only the description provided by a witness or victim? This can be done by using a process known as 'electronic facial identification technique' (E-fit), which is a technological advance on the original facial composite that was produced by police artists to reconstruct a suspect's face from witness descriptions. Alternatively it can be reconstructed using the procedure known as photofit.

FORENSIC ANTHROPOLOGY AND ARCHAEOLOGY

The forensic anthropologist and archaeologist are the experts who look at human remains that are too decomposed for a pathologist to examine – after all, once the flesh has gone, there is little left for the pathologist to examine.

The work of forensic anthropologists and archaeologists is most valuable when examining mass graves resulting from conflict, such as the wars in Rwanda and Kosovo, from terrorist attacks such as September 11, or natural disasters such as the 2004 tsunami. Closer to home these experts will also be called upon following the discovery of skeletal remains, to ascertain if they are human, and if they are, to help establish the sex and age of the body.

The role of the anthropologist is concerned with the examination and identification of the human remains, whereas the archaeologist has experience in recovering the body and in careful excavation of the burial site. Forensic archaeologists have continued to be an instrumental part of the investigation into the Moors Murders committed by Ian Brady and Myra Hindley, in the search for the missing body of their victim, Keith Bennett.

ENTOMOLOGY

When fifteen-year-old Karen Price's skeletal remains were discovered rolled in a carpet in Cardiff in 1989, entomologists attended the scene and from studying insect eggs were able to ascertain that she had been dead for ten years. She was identified following the clay facial reconstruction produced by Richard Neave, and DNA comparisons taken from her remains and samples taken from her parents.

Entomology is the study of insects, which has so much relevance to murder investigations because insects can reveal whether the body has been moved since death, as well as providing an approximation as to how long the person has been dead.

As with any attempt to ascertain time of death, entomology is subject to a number of variables, but it works on the basis that certain insect colonies mature in cycles that can be measured. Insect cycles differ according to seasons, geographical location and weather.

Buried bodies that have traces of larvae, eggs and pupae provide a strong indication that they have been killed elsewhere above ground and then buried, as insects will not burrow underground to feed on a cadaver, with the exception of the appropriately named coffin fly. The presence of larvae and suchlike from blowflies on buried bodies can help investigators ascertain how long the body was left above ground before it was buried.

FORENSIC ODONTOLOGY

A forensic odontologist can help identify human remains by comparing their teeth to ante-mortem dental records. They will also be able to estimate an approximate age of the deceased, and may be called upon to analyse bite marks. The notorious American serial killer, Ted Bundy, murdered over thirty women. His many offences, which he committed throughout the 1970s, included burglary, kidnap, rape, sodomy, necrophilia, and escaping lawful custody – twice.

An indisputable piece of evidence that matched Bundy to one of his victims was a bite mark that he made on the left buttock of a young woman he murdered, Lisa Levy. She had been raped, strangled and sustained head injuries in 1978 whilst sleeping at her university lodgings in Florida. At the same

Bite marks in an apple.

time he murdered another young woman and assaulted a further two. Investigators photographically recorded the bite mark, and this impression was later conclusively linked to Bundy's own teeth, with the odontologist able to conclude that the mark on Levy had been left following a double bite by Bundy. The deranged serial killer was sentenced to death and executed in January 1989.

FORENSIC PSYCHOLOGY

Forensic psychologists are the experts police turn to in an attempt to help profile a killer, so they can ascertain the type of person they are looking for and also understand what motivates them. When horrific crimes such as murder and rape are committed, the first question people ask is 'why'. It is human nature to want to know what has motivated the offender, so that people can come to terms with what has happened. After all, as crime writers we are expected to provide the answer, or what is the point of the story?

Psychological theories are based around the long-standing nature/nurture debate as to whether people are genetically predisposed to be evil, or whether their own experiences, particularly situations they have been exposed to during childhood, have had such an impact that they are driven to become killers.

It is also well documented that damage to the frontal lobe of the brain can cause people to act more irrationally and aggressively than they would have prior to sustaining such an injury. Therefore, if someone born with frontal lobe impairment acts in a violent or anti-social manner regardless of consequences, can we expect them to be culpable for their actions?

One of Britain's most renowned forensic psychologists, Paul Britton, worked on a number of high profile murder cases involving Fred and Rosemary West, and the killers of Jamie Bulger. If you are interested in forensic psychology, and would like to learn more about the processes and methods involved in profiling murder suspects, then I can thoroughly recommend two books written by the eminent Paul Britton: *The Jigsaw Man* and *Picking up the Pieces*.

OTHER AGENCIES: COURT

The final stage of any criminal investigation takes place in court. This is when crime scene investigators produce their witness statements, and usually take no further part in the proceedings unless they are required to give evidence. However, it is the beginning of a long journey for the investigation and legal teams, who have to gather and present all the evidence and surmise the indictable offence to determine in which court the case will be held.

At this stage the defence will meticulously comb through the entire contemporaneous note taking, the careful and meticulous exhibiting and record keeping of exhibit movements, the scene logs, forensic and arrest strategies and interviews in the hope of finding any loophole, evidential weakness or opportunity to discredit any part of the investigation.

The court process itself is long and protracted, and involves so many different players that it is not possible to detail it all here; however, I would like to cover a few areas that may prove beneficial to your writing, or at least give you an awareness of where to extend future research.

Prosecution and Defence

Think of the courtroom as a football pitch with two teams (prosecution and defence), the referee (judge) and the spectators (jury). The prosecution are the side responsible for gathering all the evidence to prove the defendant (in this case the football!) guilty. The defence will aim to prove that the defendant is innocent, and will question each and every stage of the investigation, providing allegedly plausible explanations for any evidence or witness statements given.

Crown Prosecution Service

Established in 1986, the Crown Prosecution Service (CPS) governs England and Wales in deciding whether there is sufficient evidence to result in a realistic prospect of conviction, and then the public interest test is applied.

Ireland and Scotland are governed separately, by the Court Service of Ireland and the Scottish Courts. The CPS is headed by the Director of Public Prosecutions (DPP), and as well as deciding on which criminal cases should be brought to trial, it also provides legal advice to the police and other agencies.

Types of Court

A number of courts may be relevant to your storyline, depending on its nature and the actions of your characters. The various types of court are as follows:

Magistrate's court: All criminal cases are heard at a magistrate's court. Where the offence is too severe for the magistrate to award sentence, or if the case requires the defendant to be tried by jury, then the magistrate will defer the case to the Crown Court. A magistrate's court typically consists of three Justices of the Peace, who will deal with road traffic offences and minor assaults.

Crown Court: The judge presides over proceedings and the evidence is heard by twelve members of the jury, who are randomly selected members of the public. On hearing evidence from both the prosecution and defence, the judge will summarize proceedings and then advise the jury to retire and decide whether the defendant should be found guilty or not guilty.

Coroner's court: The role of the coroner's court has already been discussed in Chapter 2 – establishing if a death is suspicious.

Military court: This court deals with the court martial of military personnel, who if found guilty will be awarded suitable punishment as defined by military law.

Civil court: This court deals with non-criminal cases, where one party believes their rights have been infringed by another party. The parties can be businesses or individuals seeking to recoup lost finances, or neighbour and landlord issues disputing access to property or land.

Court of appeal: A defendant sentenced by magistrates may appeal their sentence to be heard at Crown Court. Where a defendant has been tried at Crown Court, they may appeal to a higher judiciary, with the final court of appeal being heard at the Supreme Court.

Youth court: This is similar to magistrate's court, but the sessions are held in private and deal with the interests of youths aged between ten and seventeen.

PUBLIC ORGANIZATIONS

Below is a list of other public organizations for you to consider when writing, as they are often involved at some point during a criminal investigation, depending on the circumstances. This list is not exhaustive, but can include the following:

- National Crime Agency
- National Health Service
- UK Border Agency
- British Transport Police

- HM Revenue and Customs
- Department for Work and Pensions
- Department of Health
- National Crime Agency
- Health and Safety Executive
- HM Prison Service
- Probation

EMERGENCY SERVICES

This list includes the other emergency services and similar organizations whose priority is to serve and keep the public safe, sometimes to the detriment of their own health and safety.

- Paramedics
- Doctors
- Nurses
- Fire brigade (including the Hazardous Materials Team)
- Search and Rescue
- Royal National Lifeboat Institute
- Coastguard
- Military
- Bomb disposal

LOCAL AUTHORITIES

This final list includes departments within the local authority, which also become involved in criminal investigations.
- Social Services
- Housing
- Benefits
- Education
- Waste disposal
- Trading Standards
- Environmental Health

And finally, it would not be possible to write a book that features death in so much detail without acknowledging the wonderful work carried out by undertakers and other individuals employed in the funeral business. It is safe to say that, like crime writers, they will always be in demand.

Acknowledgements

This book would never have happened without the support of some amazing people whom I am blessed to have in my life. First, and most importantly, my husband Gary, who has been instrumental in motivating, handholding, coffee or wine (delete as applicable), fetching and feeding me. He has not only encouraged me throughout, but has also done everything possible to allow me the time to write.

My daughters, Sophie and Elissa, deserve an extra special mention for supplying lots of kisses and cuddles and for being very helpful. Gary and the girls have been invaluable in supporting me and metaphorically kicking me up the backside: thank you to all three of you, I love you all.

Thanks go to mum and my mum- and dad-in-law for also consistently encouraging me, helping out with childcare, and generally being three wonderful parents. I could never have coped and kept my sanity as a CSI or a writer for as long as I have without Gary and my parents keeping me going when I've needed it.

Likewise my friends, in particular Jeanette! And of course, in ever loving memory of my wonderful Gran – a copy of this is going in our bookcase – I miss you every day and hope I've made you proud.

Special thanks go to all my friends in the writing community, including fellow poets and writers from Swanwick Writer's Summer School, who gave me the idea to write this book in the first place. Also to my friends and colleagues at Greater Manchester Police – thanks for the experience, opportunities and so many precious memories – here's to many more, and please stay safe.

And finally, my thoughts and respect go to the friends and families of all the victims of crime I have ever dealt with, and those in the cases I have mentioned throughout this book. I pray that all of you find the justice, peace and serenity you deserve.

Glossary

ACC	assistant chief constable
ACPO	Association of Chief Police Officers
ANPR	automatic number plate recognition
ARU/V	armed response unit/vehicle
Boss	terminology for addressing an inspector or above
brief	solicitor
CID	Criminal Investigation Department
CJA	Criminal Justice Act
coke	cocaine
CPA	crime pattern analysis
CPS	Crown Prosecution Service
CRB	Criminal Records Bureau
CSE	crime scene examiner
CSI	crime scene investigator
CSM	crime scene manager
DC	detective constable
DCC	deputy chief constable
DCI	detective chief inspector
DCS	detective chief superintendent
Dibble	slang name for police
DNA	deoxyribonucleic acid
DS	detective sergeant
DVI	disaster victim identification
E-fit	electronic facial identification technique
EOD	Explosive Ordnance Disposal
ESDA	electrostatic detection apparatus
ESLA	electrostatic lifting apparatus
Feds	Americanized slang meaning police
FEL	fingerprint enhancement laboratory
FIO	force intelligence officer
FLO	family liaison officer
FME	forensic medical examiner
FSS	Forensic Science Service
gear	drugs
GRIM	glass refractive index measurement
GSR	gunshot residue (also known as FDR – firearms discharge residue)
HMCS	Her Majesty's Court Service
HMIC	Her Majesty's Inspector Constabulary
HOLMES	Home Office Large Major Enquiry System
HSE	Health and Safety Executive
IAFIS	integrated automatic fingerprint identification system
ID	identity
ident	positive fingerprint match
ident1	National Finger and Palm Print Identification Database

IED	improvised explosive device
IPCC	Independent Police Complaints Commission
ISO	International Standards Organisation
JP	Justice of the Peace
LCN	low copy number DNA
Ma'am	terminology for addressing female inspector or above
MG11	witness statement
misper	missing person
MIT	major incident team
MLP	multi locus probe
MO	modus operandi
NABIS	National Ballistics Intelligence Service
NAFIS	National Automatic Fingerprint Identification System
NCIS	National Criminal Intelligence Service
NCS	National Crime Squad
NDNA	National DNA Database
NPIA	National Police Improvement Agency
PACE	Police and Criminal Evidence Act 1984
PCR	polymerase chain reaction
PCSO	police community support officer
piece	firearm
PM	post mortem/autopsy
PNC	Police National Computer
POI	person of interest
POLSA	police search adviser
PPE	personal protective equipment
PSU	Police Support Unit
refs	refreshment break
RPU	Road Policing Unit
RTC	road traffic collision
RVP	rendezvous point
scrote	unpleasant offender
SGM	Second Generation Multiplex
SICAR	shoeprint image capture and retrieval
SIO	senior investigating officer
SLP	single locus probe
smack	heroin
SOCA	Serious and Organised Crime Agency
SOCO	scenes of crime officer
SSM	scientific support manager
SSOU	Serious Sexual Offences Unit
STR	short tandem repeat
TAU	Tactical Aid Unit
TFU	Tactical Firearms Unit
TGM	Third Generation Multiplex
traps	custody suite
TSU	Technical Support Unit
USW	Underwater Search Unit
UV	ultraviolet
VCSI	volume crime scene investigator
VIPER	video identification parade electronic recording
VISOS	Violent and Sex Offenders Register
weed	cannabis

Index